My
City
Different

My City Different

A HALF-CENTURY IN SANTA FE

Betty E. Bauer

SUNSTONE PRESS
SANTA FE

On the cover:
Watercolor of East DeVargas Street, Santa Fe, by Carulo 1981

© 2004 by Betty E. Bauer.
All rights reserved.

No part of this book may be reproduced in any form or by any electronic or mechanical means including information storage and retrieval systems without permission in writing from the publisher, except by a reviewer whomay quote brief passages in a review.

Sunstone books may be purchased for educational, business, or sales promotional use. For information please write: Special Markets Department, Sunstone Press, P.O. Box 2321, Santa Fe, New Mexico 87504-2321.

Library of Congress Cataloging-in-Publication Data:
Bauer, Betty E., 1928–
  My city different: a half-century in Santa Fe / by Betty E. Bauer.
    p. cm.
  ISBN: 0-86534-421-3 (pbk.)
  1. Bauer, Betty E., 1928– 2. Santa Fe (N.M.)—Biography.
  3. Journalists—New Mexico—Santa Fe—Biography.
    I. Title.
F804.S253B38 2004
978.9'56053'092—dc22
                        2004000893

WWW.SUNSTONEPRESS.COM
SUNSTONE PRESS / POST OFFICE BOX 2321 / SANTA FE, NM 87504-2321 / USA
(505) 988-4418 / *ORDERS ONLY* (800) 243-5644 / FAX (505) 988-1025

Dedicated
to all those who contributed
to my life and times
in Santa Fe, New Mexico

This is a glimpse of Santa Fe,
New Mexico as I knew it—
and a few of the people who made it so

INTRODUCTION

The first Spaniard to travel the long, hard journey from Mexico into the land that became New Mexico was Francisco Vasquez de Coronado, a gentleman adventurer in search of gold. He made the trip in 1540-42 and found only primitive Indian adobe dwellings which, in the sun's reflection, may have resembled the golden Cities of Cibola to a more imaginative fellow, but generated only profound disappointment in Coronado.

Half a century later, Don Juan de Oñate set forth from the district of Chihuahua, Mexico in New Spain and founded the first settlement slightly north of present-day Santa Fe on the Rio Grande. He was Governor of this new land until 1608, when the Viceroy in Mexico City, displeased with Oñate's performance, forced him to resign and sent Don Pedro de Peralta to replace him.

Peralta founded the city of Santa Fe in 1610 as the capital of New Mexico, and proceeded to lay the town out in accordance with established Spanish custom.

Laid out in a Roman grid pattern, the plaza was the center or hub with all streets emanating from it. The streets, having been laid out in the first part of the 17th century, are narrow but straight. They form boxes of ever-increasing size, fanning out with regularly-spaced, parallel streets going north and south, intersecting similarly-laid streets flowing east to west, so that there is a uniformity to the center of town which is lacking in the outlying areas. Added later, the early residential streets were formed haphazardly and are inclined to wind and weave around every which way, making it easy for a newcomer to get very lost.

The small Spanish town thrived until the 1680's when the Indians of the many surrounding pueblos became fed up with their treatment by the Spaniards, particularly the Franciscan Priests, and revolted. They took the town in a bloody battle and held it until 1693 when Don Diego de Vargas marched on the city and, in a bloodless reconquest, re-established the seat of government and Spain's dominance over the new land.

Mexico declared its independence from Spain in 1821 and became a Republic in 1824. New Mexico became a part of the Republic of Mexico until, as a result of the Mexican War of 1846, the United States acquired most of New Mexico. The rest was redeemed through the Gadsden Purchase in 1853. Union troops recaptured the territory after Confederate troops held it briefly during the Civil War. Thus, four flags have flown from Santa Fe's venerable Palace of the Governors.

For two-thirds of a century, New Mexico remained a territory. Finally, in 1912, it was the last of the contiguous states to be admitted to the Union.

Santa Fe is in the northernmost part of the state and, at 7,000 feet, lies at the base of the Sangre de Cristo Mountains which rise to more than 12,000 feet. It is high desert country with broad vistas, mountains in every direction, rock formations and badlands. Tall pine, spruce and aspen grow in abundance high in the mountains, and the foothills are alive with forests of stunted piñon and juniper. It is breathtakingly beautiful country.

The state is sparsely settled with fewer than two million inhabitants which ranks it thirty-sixth among the states in population; however, its extensive land area measures more than 120,000 square miles which puts it fifth in the nation in size. Santa Fe, with a population today of about 65,000, is still a relatively small city. Its population totaled about 19,000 when I arrived in 1953 but, being neither a boom nor bust city, a steady growth rate in the two percent range has been responsible for the population increase.

Normally, Santa Fe's climate is mild, but extremes do happen. It has four distinct seasons, with winter lows near 30° and summer highs in the mid-80°s. I have known a few winters where the temperature dropped to 12° below, and summers where it rose into the high 90°s. Extreme temperatures are far more tolerable in Santa Fe than elsewhere because of the very low humidity which sits at about 13 percent most of the time, but has gone as low as 6 percent on occasion.

It is high desert, and lack of precipitation can be dire. There are years when winter snows have been generous and spring and summer rains plentiful. Then the run-off fills the reservoirs to overflowing and the desert is lush and jumping with wild flowers. In those years, the native wild life stay in the upper reaches of the mountains, the grass down below is green and bountiful, and gardens bloom with abandon. Then there are the other years when winters are warm and open, and snow doesn't come. Spring and summer rains have forsaken the land and it is brown. The grass dries up, flowers fade and die, and the mountain critters come to town in search of food and water. Magnificent deer saunter through residential grounds, plucking leaves from the trees and grazing on the remains of whatever edibles are to be found. The bears come around to gobble fruit from the few trees that are bearing and frighten the newcomers who are not in the habit of finding bears in their yards.

Santa Fe has only two major industries—tourism and government. For this reason, the town is full of small businesses, most of which depend on tourism for their survival.

It is called *The City Different* and was so named because it was strange and foreign to visitors and not remotely like any other American city. Its inhabitants also were thought to be a bit strange and different. This was in part caused by the cultural stew represented by the mix of Spaniards, Indians and Anglo Americans, seasoned with sprinkles of ex-patriot Russians, French, British, Germans and Chinese. And the lifestyle was also strange and different, being largely unrestrictive and tolerant.

Santa Fe is an inventive place, alive with creative people because newcomers, without trust accounts or other means of outside support, have to invent a way to earn a living or leave.

It is a land of contrast—a land than can be soft and seductive—a land that can be harsh and cruel.

1

I came to Santa Fe by accident in 1948. I had been with my parents and their dearest friends to a fishing resort in Colorado's Conejos Canyon just across the border from New Mexico. A day or two before we were to leave to return home to St. Joseph, Missouri, the cagey old duffer that owned the place got my father and his buddy, Lou, alone and said " You fellas ever been to Santa Fe?" They naturally said "What's that? Where's that? Why?" I say naturally because certainly no one East of the Missouri River, and not many West of it, had ever heard of Santa Fe. At any rate, he pricked their curiosity and further suggested we could see Taos on the way, then Santa Fe, then White Sands, Carlsbad Caverns, Juarez, Mexico, and so take the Southern route home. He had an ulterior motive—his daughter, a girl about my age, was staying with him during the summer and, this being August, he wanted to get her back to her mother in Lubbock, Texas in time for school. So once the men agreed we'd go that way, he suggested we take his daughter and so we did.

Santa Fe was unlike any place I'd ever been or even imagined—low-lying, sun-baked adobe buildings with parapets along the roofline out of which short wood troughs jutted at each end and sometimes toward the center, slanted slightly downward. I learned that they were called canales and drained the roof of rain and melting snow. There were no harsh edges or corners. The buildings had a sculpted quality and were uniformly brown in color, highlighted with deep blue, green or white trim around the doors and windows. Here and there were murals painted on the walls—garden scenes, Spanish dancers in elaborate costumes, and religious icons. Behind gates and arches in the walls you could glimpse effusive gardens and sometimes a fountain—little droplets of water lazily flowing from its upper tiers to the basin below and, from somewhere behind those walls, was the delicate hum of guitar and lilting Spanish lyrics flowing from some disembodied caballeros.

We went to the Pink Adobe which at that time was in Prince Patio, and what a treat to sit outdoors to eat in a garden—no flies or mosquitos. In Missouri in August we'd have been eaten alive and suffocated in the heat. And the sky was so blue, breathtakingly blue and clear and clean.

I had never missed St. Joe, but I missed Santa Fe the day we left and every day thereafter until at last in 1953 I came home.

2

I lived in a small compound off Galisteo for about a year and worked at the *New Mexican*. In those days, the paper still published a weekly Spanish Edition, *Nuevo Mexicano*, as well as the daily New Mexican. It had a staff of two. The younger member of the duo was a cute little fellow barely five feet tall named José Gallegos. José and I became good friends. I think he was attracted by my very blond hair. We'd go out after work for a beer, and one of our favorite hangouts was Frank's Bar (where the Palace Restaurant is now). Along with Frank, it was presided over by Rosie Moya—a big, jolly gal who did not suffer nonsense or fools easily.

One night we were sitting in a booth in the front part of the bar. I was facing the back part of the place which had an arched hallway that led into a rear room of some sort. I was never in there so don't know what, if anything, went on back there. I was gazing absently toward this arched opening when suddenly a gigantic woman appeared. She filled the archway. She just stood there and looked at me and said aloud, "Wellll!" Jose´ looked up, saw her and said to me, "I think it's time for us to go." I found she was not the giant it seemed she was that night. She was Margaret Williams, known by everyone as Scoop. She surely had given me the once over.

Later I met her through a friend of mine. She lived in an old cluttered adobe house on Camino Don Miguel, and she had a piano which she played beautifully. She was a strange one and reclusive. I never saw her again.

The paper threw a big Christmas party at La Posada for all the employees. Mary Rose Bradford, former wife of Roark Bradford and mother of Richard, was dating Bill Bailey, Sportswriter at the paper. He was a crusty, sarcastic son-of-a-gun but, at a party, all the Irish came through and he was a lot of fun. I think Mary Rose, who was vivacious and full of hell, brought out the best in him.

There was an old upright piano in the dining room, and Mary Rose hammered out tune after tune and sang the words in a gutsy, raucous voice. Most of us sang along.

Jim Hughes, the Advertising Manager and my immediate boss, had promoted brides, babies, beauty, friendship, Fiesta, fireworks, rodeo, ranches, races, saints, sausage and siesta in an effort to build advertising inches for the paper until he hit the really big one—his vacation issue special—also his swan song. After that issue was sold and packaged, he left. Exhausted I should think.

Emory Bahr was the General Manager, and he hired a young man from the Midwest, George Mouchette. George and I became good friends, and he recalled to me his employment interview with McKinney. Robert McKinney was the owner and publisher of the paper. George was invited to the ranch—McKinney's home—and was shown into the library by their man who was sort of a butler, gentleman's gentleman, handyman and general factorum.

George sat in an upholstered, but miserably uncomfortable, chair and waited. McKinney finally entered and sat opposite George on a couch which had a long coffee table placed in front of it. There was a rectangular-shaped box on the table. It was silver with McKinney's monogram intricately inlaid in turquoise on the lid.

McKinney asked George a question and, while George was answering, he casually opened the box which had a hinged lid. George thought he was going to have a cigarette, but instead he looked inside the box for a moment, then closed the lid.

Every time he asked George a question, he went through the same routine. Opened the box, looked inside, then closed the box.

The telephone rang in another room and McKinney's man came and called him away. George couldn't stand it—he had to know what was inside that box. He raced to the coffee table and, breathless, he opened the box. There was nothing inside, but the interior of the lid contained a mirror.

One Saturday I was having lunch at the Pink Adobe which was now housed in an old adobe on College Street (which was later changed to the Old Santa Fe Trail) across from what was then St. Michaels High School. It was summer, and I was sitting outside on the patio. At a nearby table sat an older woman with a young girl. They were chatting away, and I was happily eavesdropping. The woman fascinated me. She had an angular face with a straight acqualine nose and she wore a flat-crowned, wide-brimmed hat sort of gaucho style; dark trousers, jacket and a cream-colored blouse completed the ensemble. In a cultured, whiskey-baritone, she was asking the young woman something about her school when another woman walked up to the table and interrupted. The lady in the hat said, "Oh, Susan, I want you to meet my niece from Las Cruces."

With that tidbit of information, I marched into the office of the Society Editor, Ann Clark on Monday to find out who the woman was. I described the woman to Ann and said she had a young woman with her who was her niece from Las Cruces. "Oh," Ann said, "of course, that was Eleanor Bedell. She's one of our better local lessies."

I was stunned. I was pretty sure I had interpreted her meaning correctly, but I had never heard that term tossed out so casually. I did not know then that Santa Fe was a refuge for homosexuals and all others whose proclivities labeled them a little the other side of center.

Peach Mayer (Katherine), Mrs. Walter, was a very energetic Santa Fean. She devoted much of her life and her able executive abilities to doing good works. She was involved with the Maternal and Child Health Center, New Mexico Heart Association, and the Santa Fe Boys Club. She was forever a regent, was twice the President of the Museum of New Mexico Foundation, and served at least seven terms as President of the Santa Fe Opera Foundation. She was a very active staunch Republican. Peach was not loved by all and had made a few powerful enemies.

While I was still at the *New Mexican*, Peach Mayer's husband, Walter, shot a man back east in Iowa. It came in on the wire late at night and Dick Everet, the Managing Editor, had left for the day. The paper had been put to bed and the presses were running. Art Morgan was the only one in the news room, and he didn't have the authority to stop the presses. Dick was nowhere to be found, so the paper didn't carry the story in the Sunday edition which was the next day after the shooting. McKinney blew his top. I think he was not fond of Peach and printing that story would have given him great satisfaction. As it was, he had to be content with firing poor Dick Everet, which he did on the spot.

3

Some friends of mine, Bill and Josie, and I decided we'd do a little spying on the I AMs, a mysterious religious cult which had been kicked out of California to resettle in Santa Fe. It was known that their big meeting day was Wednesday and their temple was, we thought, easily accessible, lying as it was just off the road at the foot of the old Taos Highway. There were many stories about Mrs. Ballard, the head hancho, and her cult. They worshipped St. Germaine and were very sensitive to colors—purple was the best, but all pastels were in—red and black were the devil's colors and to be avoided at all costs. They were vegetarians—absolutely no meat, and spirits were verboten. It was rumored that they could only mate during the month of April but, if some woman was just beside herself during some other month, she could go to the big mucky-muck, Mrs. Ballard's right hand man, and be serviced. What men with a like problem did is anybody's guess.

    We parked the car up the hill away from the temple and crept down the side of the road, keeping close to the ditch. When we arrived at a good vantage point where we thought we'd be able to see the goings-on through the windows, we lay in the ditch, concealed by some tumbleweeds. Music started and we eagerly awaited action to begin. Just as there was movement inside, there was movement just inches from our hiding place. Oh, my God—it was a uniformed guard patrolling the grounds carrying a very menacing-looking shotgun. "Yipes, let me outta here," I thought, but didn't dare say a word. Shortly after, he moved off toward the other end of the grounds and you never saw three people skedaddle any faster than we did—up the hill, in the car and away.

I never had any further interest in the I AMers except one evening to note Mrs. Ballard's son in La Fonda enjoying a big steak and a bottle of wine.

Another time, Bill and Josie and I went to Taos. One of the famous early Taos painters, Bert Phillips, was Bill's great uncle, and I was to meet him. Taos was settled at the foot of the mountains which rose straight up perpendicular to the land. I found them harsh and unrelenting, not at all like Santa Fe's Sangre de Cristos which were comforting and embracing. Some thought the people of Taos felt threatened by those mountains, and that was why they were such a cliquish, churlish bunch. Whatever its cause, it seemed to me there was an undercurrent—an ill wind that permeated the town. It was really not a town at all, more a village—at that time, mid-fifties, there were probably no more than 2500 people who lived there.

Bert Phillips was an elderly gentleman, very gracious with courtly, old-fashioned manners. He was still a fine painter and I was honored to meet him. While there, I also met Lady Dorothy Brett, a titled English woman who was a part of the D. H. Lawrence saga. She was amusing, with light blue twinkling eyes and unruly white hair that was forever escaping its bondage. She, too, was a painter of some renown. I saw her many times thereafter lunching in Santa Fe at La Fonda, regaling her companions with tales of Taos goings-on.

We visited Taos Pueblo which was a sophisticatedly-constructed tri-level apartment complex built by the Indians centuries before. The Taos Indians are a handsome breed, more closely related, it is believed, to the Plains Indians, than to those of New Mexico's other Pueblos. It was there I met Jerry Mirabel. He was a canny, engaging middle-aged Indian who gave me a hard-luck story which I thought was worth the dollar he wheedled out of me. It intrigued me to have a real Indian acquaintance—that is, until about his third visit to the New Mexican to hit me up each time for another dollar.

4

The first house I owned in Santa Fe was a small studio house with a large walled garden and patio. It was down a little lane off Cerro Gordo Road. There was an adobe house with a pitched roof on Cerro Gordo at the corner where my lane turned off. It was owned and had been built by a nice youngish man who I knew only as Pedro. He lived there with his wife and several small children. A large wooden plaque had been placed above the door lintel just under where the roof peaked. In bright red large letters crudely painted, it read "LIVE AND LET LIVE."

There was a profusion of outhouses among the hills off the north side of the road. On my side, the south side, the land was flatter and sloped down toward the Santa Fe Canyon and river far below. Either there were no outhouses on my side of the road or they had been artfully concealed.

It was 1956 and Santa Fe still had a bus—as far as I know, it was the only bus route left. It was the Canyon Road, Cerro Gordo route so, coming from town, it followed Palace Avenue to Canyon Road, east on Canyon Road to just before it reached the Randall Davey property where the road made a wide curve to the north, then to the west where it became Cerro Gordo. A Mr. Gustafsson lived just beyond the junction on the south side of the road. He was Greta Garbo's brother, and she was a frequent, rarely seen visitor. The road wound around the hills and eventually went past my lane and ended back on Palace Avenue and thus into town. One day a friend of mine was driving on Palace and had just approached its intersection with Cerro Gordo when she spotted a woman trudging toward town. It was a cold, blustery day, so she stopped the car and asked the woman if she'd like a ride. The woman got in the car and my friend recognized her, but didn't ever let on that she knew her hitchhiker was the great Greta Garbo.

Neither Canyon Road nor Cerro Gordo yet had been paved so it was a dusty ride on the non-air-conditioned bus. One time I was riding the bus on the afternoon run and the bus driver stopped in front of a house set up the hill away from the road. The driver got out of the bus, went to the mail box at the side of the road, took out the mail, trudged up the hill to the house, opened the door and set the mail inside. I wondered if it was his house, but I later learned that a little old lady lived there who was badly crippled with arthritis, and that he stopped every day to take her mail to her.

Another time I got on the bus and there was a large box of groceries sitting in the well next to the driver. I assumed he'd done some shopping for his wife, but discovered that was not so when he made a stop in front of a house on Canyon Road, honked the horn and put the box by the side of the road. As we were pulling away, a young woman came out of the house followed by a couple of toddlers, picked up the groceries and marched back into the house with the groceries and the two young ones. She had no car and this was the way she got her groceries.

Around and about Cerro Gordo, there was a dapper little man who was always astride a beautiful chestnut horse and, on the ground by his side, a lively cocker spaniel of almost the identical color as the horse tagged along. I asked a neighbor who he was and she laughed and said, "Oh, that's *El Borracho*. He's the keeper of the horses." It was still okay to have horses and, for that matter, all manner of domesticated animals—sheep, goats, pigs, chickens—on Cerro Gordo, and it was *El Borracho*'s job to see that the horses all stayed in their own corrals. I thought *El Borracho* was his title, sort of like the Major Domo of the ditches, but it wasn't. Translated it means "the drunk"

Well, there was no doubt that *El Borracho* earned his name. Driving home from work along Canyon Road, many's the time I would see that beautiful chestnut horse with his cocker friend of the same color waiting patiently in front of the Canyon Road Bar.

One bitter cold night, I was coming home from dinner at The Chinaman's downtown (it was the New Canton, but we all called it The Chinaman's) when, as I started to turn off Cerro Gordo into my lane, my headlights caught the chestnut cocker spaniel sitting by the side of the ditch. Oh, oh, where's *El Borracho*? I stopped the car and got out and went over to the ditch—there lay *El Borracho* on a bed of ice. I didn't know whether he was passed out or dead. I got back in the car and raced down the lane to my house and the phone. I called the police and told them *El Borracho* was in the ditch. They all knew him and came and got him and the little cocker spaniel. They were kept the night in a nice warm jail; and the next morning when I went to work, there he was sitting astride his chestnut horse with the faithful little dog following along.

5

I believe I met Claude James at a poker party. A bunch of us would get together on Saturday nights and play penny-ante. Claude loved to play cards and someone invited her to join the group. Claude's father was the Managing Editor of the New York Times. Her mother was a pretty, petite French woman. Claude had been raised in France and spoke French fluently, and English with one of those delightful accents that Americans love. She arrived in Santa Fe wearing a perky little navy blue hat, navy and white dress, blue pumps and white gloves. She was five feet tall and svelte at the time. Her traveling companion and friend was Allison Abott.

When I met her, her figure had blossomed. She wore men's trousers, a tweed jacket, open-necked white shirt and very dirty oxfords. She had long since forsaken Allison and, although she and Happy Krebs were still partners in The Clip Joint, a successful dog-grooming operation, they no longer lived together. Happy had been married to Peter Krebs and, when Claude moved in with Happy, Peter moved out. Years later, Happy ended up with Allison, and Peter became very friendly with Mike James, Claude's brother. Santa Fe was like that—musical chairs all around.

Claude decided she was going to have a party and she wanted me to come. It was late April, but still cold and windy; and Santa Feans, bored with winter and hibernating, were ready to party. Claude lived in a fair-size derelict of a house. It was full of dogs, mostly big standard poodles, and she was a lousy—really non-existent—housekeeper. The morning of the party, Claude called me in a panic. "My house—*merd* everywhere, the dogs you know—You'll have to have the party at your house!" "But, Claude, I don't know these people and how many? 16!, you say—my house is tiny—where can I put 16 people?" I wailed—"I can't do it—You'll have to find someone else." Well, she wasn't about to find someone else—it was going to be at my house period and, furthermore, she'd already called everyone and told them it would be at my house and how to get there. "Don't worry," she said, "I'll bring the food and the liquor." "But," I said, "how will I know who these people are if some of them arrive before you get here?" She read me her list and some I knew by sight, although I'd never met any of them—one pair I'd never seen or even heard of. "How will I know those two?" I complained. She replied, "Moya Canning is the most beautiful woman you've ever seen and Cecily Cunha is the biggest woman you've ever seen. They'll arrive in a yellow Cadillac."

There was no mistaking those two even without the yellow Cadillac. Moya Canning was in her mid-fifties, an ex-patriot Brit, about my height, 5'6", and slender but full-figured. A halo of silvery white hair framed her exquisite patrician features. She was obviously a woman of the world—a commanding presence—a woman used to having it all.

Cecily Cunha was equally stunning. She was part Hawaiian and part Portuguese—tall, a 6 footer, with wide shoulders like a football player encased in his protective padding. Her figure was V-shaped—wide shoulders, narrow waist and slim hips. She had a mop of naturally curly hair and a perpetual suntan. She wore a full-length mink and teetered on spike heels, like an enormous grizzly bear on roller skates. She had been an Olympic swimmer.

Cecily had come to Santa Fe before the war with an escaped white Russian, the Countess Zena DeRossin. She bought Rancho Ancon out in Pojoaque, about 20 miles north of Santa Fe, which she and Zena ran as a sort of dude ranch playground. Parties were frequent and the guests many. Sometimes the party moved on for dinner and dancing at El Nido, a roadside restaurant and bar in Tesuque, a village just north of Santa Fe.

One memorable evening when things were going full tilt at El Nido, Fritzy Bard, another White Russian, a major in the WACS, and Zena DeRossin were talking animatedly in Russian when the FBI descended. Santa Fe was infested with agents during the war and for some years afterward because of Los Alamos. Poor Fritzy almost lost her commission and ended up in the brig over that one, but it was finally all straightened out when the FBI learned it was just innocent chitchat between two ex-patriot Russians who had barely escaped that country with their lives.

El Nido was run by the sure hand of Charlie Besre and the eagle eye of his wife, Mimi. Mimi employed her eagle eye at the cash register and kept the other eye on her husband, Charlie, who was known to have a weakness for les femmes.

El Nido was very popular. The food was exceptional, the bar generous, and it had one of only two dance floors handy to Santa Fe—the other was La Fonda.

6

La Fonda was still a Harvey House when I first knew it, and the waitresses wore the same kind of uniforms that they wore in the Judy Garland movie, albeit slightly modified. A very handsome Taos Indian hung around La Fonda—Old Joe, we called him. He'd let you take his picture for 25 cents, and I doubt there was a tourist that visited Santa Fe that didn't have a shot of Old Joe tucked away in an album somewhere.

At that time, Shorty, dressed in a crisp white uniform, patrolled the streets around the Plaza with his cart, broom and dust pan. Nary the smallest scrap of paper escaped his broom. No one seemed to know his name or for whom he worked, but he certainly kept the Plaza clean.

La Fonda was so other-worldly that, upon entering, you felt that you had walked into a picture from a history book depicting another era. The floors were gleaming dark red tile. Heavy ceiling beams were incised with simple Indian geometrics which were painted in earth tones of amber, turquoise and red, as was all the wooden trim. Huge canvases painted by Gerald Cassidy hung from the smoothly-sculpted adobe walls. B.B. Dunn (Brian Boru Dunn) presided over all from his chair prominently placed in the lobby with a clear view of the entrance. He was a journalist and interviewed all comers whom he found intriguing, be they princess or pauper.

The furniture in La Fonda was massive, made and hand-carved by native artisans. The guest rooms had little corner beehive fireplaces and, on a chilly evening, they would be laid with piñon boughs to bring cheerful warmth to the rooms and waft their fragrance throughout the downtown.

B.B. Dunn was a slight man, bent a little with age. He had very pale white skin, little beady eyes behind bifocals, and a prominent, very long, skinny nose which reminded me of a proboscis on a hummingbird. In fact, he reminded me of a hummingbird, hurrying along, flittering to and fro whenever he wasn't holding forth from his chair in La Fonda. He wore a very wide-brimmed hat, as large as a small umbrella, to shield his skin from the sun, and was frequently dressed all in white—a costume reminiscent of the Mexican peon uniform. He lived at the corner of Acequia Madre and Garcia Street in a cassita, part of an old adobe compound. In his house, a narrow archway shaped like a svelte hour glass led from the living room to the bathroom. He had an aversion to big women, did not want them hanging around, and this was his way of discouraging them.

There were a number of remittance men and some women in Santa Fe. Orphaned by their East Coast families in every way except financially, they had come West at the behest of their families because, for one reason or another, they had become a source of embarrassment. A favorite story among Santa Feans was the joke about the New Yorker whose wife had begun to behave peculiarly. The situation had gotten so bad that he was ashamed to take her out in public, yet he loved her dearly just the way she was and didn't want her to change, so he consulted a psychiatrist. He explained his problem and confessed to the doctor his great love for his wife in spite of her strange behavior and begged the doctor for a solution. The great man thought for a moment, sighed and said, "I'll tell you what to do. Take your wife to Santa Fe because there nobody will know the difference."

One of Santa Fe's remittance men was Horace Aiken who lived in a suite at La Fonda. It was said that, at one time, he had been a history professor. He was a tall, portly gentleman who was easily recognizable among the casually-dressed populace, because he always wore a bowler hat, a morning coat, dove gray vest, matching spats (long after they were passe) and shoes that glistened with polish. He carried a walking stick and he walked for miles every morning. He could be seen as far as the eastern limit of Canyon Road, away west on Alameda, and sometimes north, high on Artists Road that led up the mountain to Hyde Park.

He was very solemn and correct and always tipped his hat to the ladies. He was also a painter—quite a good one it became known when his excellent portrait of B.B. Dunn was hung in La Fonda's lobby above B.B.'s favorite chair.

7

Canyon Road veered off Paseo de Peralta to the east toward the mountains and, until the late 50's, had been mostly residential, although there were splotches of commercialism. There was a grocery and bar at 656, Gormley's grocery, and the Canyon Road Bar, a little way farther up the road just beyond the intersection with Camino del Monte Sol. Spotted here and there were artists' studios/galleries.

Eleanor Bedell was one of the first to move her store from downtown Sena Plaza to Canyon Road. She called her place simply The Shop and offered trash to treasure. She was quickly followed by Kay Stephens and her Santa Fe shirts which were expensive reproductions of the Mexican wedding shirt, Kathryn Kenton's ladies boutique, and Abacus Bookstore.

The big change came to Canyon Road with the opening of Claude's bar and restaurant about 1956. She had Jacques Cartier, who had an eye for style, to design the interior. A long, handsome bar dominated the front room where you entered. There were stools at the bar and two or three small tables against the wall opposite.

I remember John Crosby sitting alone at the bar, probably dreaming of plans for his Santa Fe Opera. Several of us were sitting at one of the small tables. The phone, which hung on the front wall next to the door, began ringing—the one behind the bar was ringing. too, but the bartender had gone to the cellar to fetch a special bottle of imported wine so there was no one to answer. We all shouted in unison, "John, answer the phone!" He looked at us and, slightly dazed, got up and answered the phone. It was a patron who wanted a reservation. John, straight-faced, listened, hung up and, without a word, walked back to the bar and wrote the information down on a cocktail napkin which he later gave to the bartender.

The large square room beyond the bar was the dining room with tables around the perimeter and a small dance floor in the center. The tables were clothed in white with small vases of bright fresh flowers in the center. An enormous fireplace occupied most of the far wall opposite the bar. Tongues of flame lazily crept up amongst the piñon logs nestled in the huge grate, issuing a cheery welcome to the diners.

Claude was an accomplished French cook. It was there that I was introduced to escargot. Coming from Missouri, I had not been exposed to that particular delicacy. "Snails!" I cried, shocked and horrified. Finally, I was persuaded to try them. Gingerly, I plucked one from its shell and, with great misgiving, tasted the rubbery critter. Well!!! They were certainly missing something in Missouri, and I became an immediate convert.

Claude's became immensely popular and was frequented by all who were anyone or who aspired to be, including Governor John Simms, Mayor Leo Murphy, State Senators, doctors, lawyers and much of the gay population.

Midway of an evening, Claude would appear in the dining room dressed in one of Kay Stephens' creations, long full skirt of heavy white cotton with a matching wedding shirt. She'd give the trio...piano, bass and violin—a sign and they would play the opening bars of La Vien Rose. Claude, her throaty voice suggestive of Marlene Dietrich, would sing in French. The audience loved it and her, and she'd follow with a couple more French songs. When Claude wanted to be, she could be exceedingly charming. She could also be a bitch.

John Crosby's opera opened during the summer of 1957. Little did we realize that it was destined to become internationally famous or that it would change Santa Fe forever.

John Levert, a tall, blond Louisianan from New Orleans, was sugar rich and owned a vast ranch just north of town off the Taos Highway. John and his friend and partner, a Dutchman named Hendrik ter Weele had purchased the Dockwiller property, a spread of 550 acres, in 1939. They built a fabulous ranch house with many guest rooms and called it San Juan Ranch, which they ran as a guest ranch until 1956.

The ranch was on the west side of the road among the foothills and faced the Sangre de Cristo mountains to the east. Farther to the west lay the Jemez range and enthralling sunsets which, after misty evenings, were reflected in incredibly gorgeous rainbows over the Sangres. This setting, John Crosby decided, was ideal for his opera, and a purchase was arranged. So the Santa Fe Opera, which many thought was John Crosby's pipedream, was on its way to becoming reality.

In retrospect, the first house was very small, but elegant. It seated only 482, and all of the seating was open to the elements. The first rows were box seats of comfortable chrome and laced vinyl, followed by rows of seasoned timber benches topped with thick blue cushions. Redwood fences hugged by stately poplars protected the audience somewhat from the night air, but not enough, and there was no roof for the audience. We wore winter clothes, including heavy coats, took blankets and thermos bottles full of black, heavily-spiked coffee to ward off the cold.

The redwood stage and outspread wooden walls supported the roof at its rear, which then canted upward to be braced at the sides by six pillars. It was fitted with a series of baffles to reflect sound from the orchestra to the performers. Behind the orchestra pit and in front of the box seats lay a raised, curved pool with the water bouncing the sound to the audience. It was an acoustical marvel.

Sliding panels at the rear of the stage opened to the piñon-covered hills and the western sky which many a time produced a full moon or loud roll of thunder as if on cue.

From its first performance to a packed house, the Santa Fe Opera was a smashing success. Distinguished for its stunning productions, superlative performances, skillfully-designed sets and gorgeous costumes, it soon attracted opera buffs from around the world.

The original house burned to the ground in 1967, but from its ashes there arose a larger, more magnificent house which today seats more than four times as many patrons as the original house. The high standards set in that original house from its opening night have not only been upheld, but more often than not have been surpassed.

Because of the Opera's excellence, its reputation put Santa Fe on the map and the small town, isolated from reality for 400 years, abruptly met the 20th Century.

8

In the 1960s, urban renewal came to Santa Fe and the town spruced up. Gone was the ugly intersection at Sandoval and Alameda known as five points—five streets that met at the intersection where, in the middle, a small island housed a liquor store. And gone were the tumbledown adobe shacks that bordered West DeVargas and faced the Santa Fe River. Bill Lumpkins and his crew had created from their shells an utterly charming, very Santa Feish facade with spiffy whitewashed interiors abutted by quaint courtyards. The entire block became highly desirable office space.

A new hotel went up on Sandoval, the Hilton. Built in approved territorial style, it cleaned up that street and the cross street which was lower San Francisco. The low-lying adobes that lined that part of San Francisco had provided many Santa Fe gentlemen with an evening of sport—gambling and girls. The Santa Fe Styles Committee ruled that the old bordellos were of historic value and could not be demolished, so instead they were restored and rehabilitated into more acceptable business enterprises.

The Plaza received a face lift. Portales were added where there were none. The ancient adobe Palace of the Governors, now a museum, which had given birth to the Ben Hur saga when Lew Wallace was Governor, was the oldest public building in continuous use in the United States. It was replastered, its vigas and canales were repaired, and the doors and window trim were freshly painted. Facades of the buildings around the Plaza were remodeled and many were replastered an adobe color to make them look more in keeping with what we had begun to call Santa Fe style. Even the four streets which enclosed the Plaza were torn up and redone, inlaid with brick.

And the Plaza itself was rejuvenated. The unsightly 12-inch-high curbs, which had provided seating for many a weary onlooker, were torn out and replaced with those of regulation height. The center part was redesigned with new trees added, grassy areas sodded, and large pinkish-red slabs of flagstone were laid to form islands on which were placed benches with wood seats and white, intricately filigreed metal backs.

Although Santa Fe had been prettied and polished, its flavor and mystique, for the time being, had been preserved. This was due in no small part to the stubborn refusal of its citizens to change their ways and to the newcomers who followed in our wake.

John Crosby's opera had introduced Santa Fe to a certain moneyed and cultured group, particularly from the East Coast, but these people came for the season. Few stayed.

But once the door was open and the community no longer isolated, the word got around and a select few were beginning to discover the quaintness of Santa Fe, the beauty of its land and the softness of its climate. Some stayed.

9

A number of years after John Crosby's dream had come true and the Santa Fe Opera had made its debut, two others had a dream that was destined to further change Santa Fe. It would bring art connoisseurs and many others to Santa Fe and turn the sleepy little town into one of the major art markets in the United States. Their dream became reality when, in 1972, the first issue of *The Santa Fean Magazine* rolled off the presses; and Betty Bauer and Marian Love, its founders, editors and publishers, began their trek into Santa Fe legend.

Marian Love had come to Santa Fe in 1943 with her three little boys—six-year-old John, Fred who was four, and Ralph not yet two. She was a New Yorker, had worked for *Time/Life*, and had come west because John was an asthmatic. Marian was a very pretty, lively, outgoing girl and much in demand for Santa Fe's many parties.

I met Marian during the summer of 1955 when, being briefly out of work because I'd left the *New Mexican* in a huff, I was waiting tables for Marcia Gilbertson who had a small bistro downtown in Prince Patio; and Marian, to help out and earn a few extra bucks, was doing the same. Marian was always on-call to help when someone started a new business or unexpectedly ran short of help during a busy season.

Through the ensuing years, we saw each other at parties and would pass in our cars with mutual smiles and waves but, having gone to work for the State, I was out of the center of activity in Santa Fe.

One Saturday in 1968, I had sold my house—this one being the third I had owned in Santa Fe—and was packing, preparing to move to a smaller place I'd bought in Casa Solana, when a friend of mine stopped by and asked me if I was going to the Opera Tea that afternoon. I had forgotten that it was to be held that Saturday and I said, "Oh, I don't think so. I really should pack." She replied, "Why don't you go. It will do you good and you can pack tomorrow." After she left, I thought, "Maybe I will go. She's right, I can pack tomorrow."

At the tea, which was held on the grounds at the opera ranch across the road from the theatre, I ran into a number of acquaintances. Then I spotted Marian, whom I hadn't seen in some time. She was with Carrie Kelly. I raced over to them and Marian threw her arms around me and kissed me, as did Carrie. Santa Fe was a very kissy town. I asked them to have dinner with me at El Nido. Carrie had other plans, but Marian said she'd go. That was the beginning of a lifelong friendship and collaboration.

First we had a little advertising agency—big talents, but small pickings. There weren't many businesses in Santa Fe that thought they needed or could afford someone to do their promotions. After a few years of near starvation, we decided to bite the bullet and see if we could launch a magazine. How naive we were—we didn't have a sou between us.

There wasn't much reading material available for visitors to learn about the town—only one publication, La Tourista, an 8 1/2 x 5 1/2 pamphlet that carried a little advertising and a few trite and often inaccurate paragraphs about Santa Fe and its environs.

We knew Santa Fe well and we were both writers—the hitch was, to fund our endeavor, we had to have advertising which meant one or both of us had to go out and sell it. Marian adamantly refused, so that left me. I can't say I was thrilled with the prospect of pounding the pavement. I had done some selling before, but I didn't enjoy it. I was still pretty shy and the idea of approaching people I didn't know or, worse, those I did know filled me with anxiety. But I knew, if we were to have this magazine, I had to do it. And not only did I have to sell an intangible (we didn't even have a mock-up), but I would have to collect on the spot to get enough money to pay the printer.

And so it began. We wrote about Santa Fe through the voices of its people, and we told their stories. We told about their unusual houses and hidden gardens. We spoke of the zesty food, the continental cuisine, and the strangely-unique restaurants. We promoted the artists and the galleries. The magazine grew and grew, as did the town. And the more we talked of art, the more artists and galleries migrated to Santa Fe until Santa Fe had become a renowned art center.

By the turn of the century, the beginning of the 20th, artists began to discover Santa Fe. One of the first painters of note to arrive was Joseph Henry Sharp. Shortly thereafter came Warren Rollins (whose towering, majestic paintings of Indians still hang on the walls at Bishop's Lodge), Sheldon Parsons, William Penhallow Henderson, Gerald Cassidy, Robert Henri and John Sloan. Many others came early in the century, including Gustave Baumann, Eugenie Shounard, and the suave, handsome Randall Davy, who loved fast cars and horses. Davy painted many scenes of jockeys and race horses, but his favorite subject was his wife, Bell, whom he painted over and over, usually nude. *Los Cincos Pintores* (the five painters)—Will Shuster, Jozef Bakos, Fremont Ellis, Willard Nash and Walter Mruk—came at about the same time, and all built adobe houses and studios on Camino del Monte Sol. The natives called them "The five nuts in adobe huts."

Will Shuster, Jozef Bakos and Fremont Ellis were still very much alive when I arrived in Santa Fe. Although Will Shuster was a good painter and did some fine etchings, he is best remembered for his creation of *Zozobra*, the giant effigy of gloom, which is burned every year to signify the end of gloom and the beginning of Fiesta. Joe Bakos was a dead ringer for the Kentucky Colonel, Colonel Sanders. One year when my uncle was visiting, we were downtown and my uncle nudged me and said, "Hey, Betty. Look, here comes the Kentucky

Colonel. I wonder what he's doing in Santa Fe?" he mused aloud. I looked to where he nodded, laughed and said, "Jack, that's no Kentucky Colonel, that's a Santa Fe painter, Joe Bakos."

Fremont Ellis had a jaunty stride and a ready smile. He was a fine painter—the best of the five, I think. Although he has gone topside since, his daughter, Bambi, carries his remaining work in her gallery.

10

Among the Santa Fe painters I knew, there were a few whose eccentricities outshone the others. One was Alfred Morang, who painted abstract landscapes using generous layers of oils and sketched local call girls in a manner similar to Toulouse-Lautrec. He also painted murals on the walls of a Canyon Road bar in exchange for his daily ration. When the walls needed a new coat of paint, the owner had the murals concealed behind slatted rough wood screens to protect and save them. Alfred reminded me somewhat of Charlie Chaplin. He was a slight man and always wore a hat and a heavy black overcoat that reached almost to his ankles. I would see him dining on the patio at the Pink Adobe in the middle of summer, overcoat intact. I wondered if he ever took it off. He and his wife, Dorothy, gave a lot of parties—if you didn't enjoy wine that came in gallon jugs, you brought your own. They were cat lovers and there were always several cats about, rubbing against a person's legs or suddenly leaping into a startled guest's lap. At one such party, a friend of mine noted a bedraggled looking old feline lying along the window ledge and went over to pet it—it was as hard as stone. Horrified, he raced over to where Alfred stood and said, "That cat—the one in the window is very dead!" Alfred nodded unperturbed and replied, "Oh, yes, poor Otto, he died a couple of weeks ago!"

Chuzo Tomatsu was a tiny Japanese. He was well under five feet tall. He had heavy eyebrows and a black handlebar moustache, worn in racing mode, that is with the handlebars turned down. His aged Model T had finally died, and he walked everywhere carrying his easel, a box of paints and a big canvas. He painted in the traditional Japanese style, mostly delicate depictions of flowers and ancient warriors. His wife, Louise, was a stout woman of Scandinavian descent who stood a foot taller than he. She worked at the State Highway Department which was located at the far southwest edge of town on the site of the old penitentiary. She pedaled her bicycle to work, to the grocery, to town, wherever she needed to go.

Tommy Macaione loved dogs and was Pied Piper to all strays. One of Santa Fe's beloved local vets, Dr. Ed Smith, displayed a large, handsome canvas on the wall of his clinic that Tommy had exchanged for dog food and shots for his menagerie. Tommy painted outdoors in the sun, the rain, the snow, warm or cold. He haunted Canyon Road and would set up his easel wherever a scene pleased him, no matter how inappropriate or inconvenient it might be to the owner of the premises. One of his favorite places was in the garden in front of the Linda McAdoo Gallery. Prospective clients would enter through the gate and Tommy would shout, "You don't need to go in there. It's very expensive. Come over here and see what I have painted for you." Needless to say, this did not altogether please Linda, but what could she do? Tommy had become a Santa Fe institution.

He had bushy, shoulder length, white with strands of gray, grizzly curly hair and a matching beard to mid-chest. It's doubtful if he ever bathed. Years before, Mike James, who was a photographer of some note, decided to make a photo essay booklet about Canyon Road and wanted to use Tommy as the focal figure. He was to wear clothes from some of the Canyon Road shops, which sent the proprietors into a tizzy. "No way is that filthy creature going to wear anything from my shop!" they roared in unison. The problem was resolved when the resourceful Mike fetched a huge tub to the back garden of one of the shops and he, with the aid of two big bruisers, gave a screaming, swearing, struggling Tommy a bath and a haircut.

He really was a good painter and his cache of lavish canvases, paintings of colorful gardens and other Canyon Road scenes, commanded good prices after his death.

The most famous painter living in the area was Georgia O'Keeffe who lived in Abique, a small village about 50 miles north of Santa Fe. I met her in 1951 when I was a guest at Ghost Ranch which, at that time, was a going ranch as well as a dude ranch. Owned by Arthur Pack and managed by Helen and Earl Vance, its many acres lay at the base of giant red rock formations for which the country in the Abique area is known.

I was an enthusiastic rider in those days and one day I asked the wrangler, upon mounting my not-so-trusty steed, "Okay, if I take that trail?" pointing to the west. He replied, "Take it, but don't get off it because Georgia O'Keeffe lives out that way. She has a shot gun and doesn't ask questions."

She deigned to come to the ranch one evening for cocktails and I'm sure the only reason she came was because she knew that Cary Grant was also a guest there, and she was after-all a female. He, by the way, was just as gracious as she was not.

She usually dressed all in black men's clothes, complete with crisp white shirt and a black string tie. She was neither friendly nor pleasant.

Years later, I saw her at a big do at one of the pueblos. She was with Juan Hamilton but, what about bowled me over, was her outfit. She was wearing a long, flowered granny dress. She must have mellowed under the tutorage of Hamilton

When the Santa Fe Music Festival was born, some courageous person was able to get O'Keeffe's consent to reproduce one of her paintings for their poster advertising the Festival. On viewing the poster for the first time, one Santa Fe wag remarked, "My God, it's a gynecologist's nightmare!" Many of her paintings appeared to be anatomically inspired.

11

During the urban renewal frenzy of the early 60's, Dick Bokum bought the corner property on Palace Avenue and Burro Alley that had included Frank's Bar. He built a two-story office building on the corner with a single story wing which was to be a restaurant where the bar had been. It had been said that was where La Doña Tules, a madam and owner of a gambling saloon during Manuel Armijo's reign as Governor the second quarter of the 19th Century, had her establishment. When the men were excavating the foundation for the new building, they found a horseshoe with a metal overlay repoussed with an elongated female leg encased in a lace stocking and flowered garter at the thigh—which seems to lend credence to the La Doña Tules theory.

Charlie and Mimi Besre had several years before sold El Nido to Ray and Irene Arias and had been waiting for an opportunity to get back in the business. This opportunity came when Dick Bokum approached them to run his restaurant which he wanted called The Palace. They, neither one, were ready for retirement and both jumped at the chance to open what was to be a very elegant new restaurant in downtown Santa Fe.

We loved to go there. The decor was gay nineties—La Doña Tules would have approved.

Patterns of lush flowers bloomed in relief from the lusty red wall paper. Comfortable red leather booths lined the perimeter of the large dining room, and the center was filled with square and round, small and large tables with small Victorian chairs of squishy pink velvet. Dainty chandeliers with frosted glass bonnets shielding the lights cast a soft, flattering pinkish glow on the diners. The food was French-inspired and consistently delicious. Charlie did the greeting and Mimi manned the cash register.

The bar was adjacent to the dining room and presided over by Robert, bartender and a black man—one of the few who lived in Santa Fe. He knew everyone and most of our secrets which he kept to himself. He built a generous drink and looked out for his clients. He tried to keep all from getting too tipsy, but he slipped up on us one night. When Marian and I left The Palace that night, we were holding each other up as we swayed across the street. When we got to the car which was parked opposite the court house, a police car sidled around the corner and stopped just as I was getting behind the wheel. "I think you ladies better let me take you home," the handsome Spanish officer said. "But officer," I protested, "I can drive just fine." "I don't think so," firmer this time. "You can leave the car here and get it in the morning." "Gee, officer, I understand your concern, but I really can drive and we're house-sitting way up on Cerro Gordo. I'll tell you what—why don't I drive and you follow me and, if I do anything wrong, you can stop me and then we'll go with you." Finally, he smiled and said, "Okay, we'll give it a try." Was I careful! He followed us all the way up Cerro Gordo. Our friend's house was near the end of the road and, when I turned off onto her driveway, I honked and stuck my hand out and waved to him. He honked back and proceeded on his way.

Santa Fe was not a dressy town. People wore what they wanted to no matter how outrageous or inappropriate—and nobody cared or even looked. During the streaking craze, Santa Fe never had any streakers because no one would have paid any attention. Even at the Opera on opening night, patrons came in all forms—from fancy gowns and furs to blue jeans and boots. This was years before the flaunting of custom became de rigueur.

Then, in the late 1960s, The Compound restaurant opened and, believe it or not, they had a dress code—just for the gentlemen, jacket and tie. They were smart enough not to include the ladies.

The restaurant was built on the grounds of what had been Mrs. McComb's compound. It was a large tract of land down a short lane, opposite Claude's bar, from Canyon Road. Mrs. McComb's home, the main building on the property, had been remodeled with the interior designed by Alexander Girard, and this became the restaurant. The property had long ago been a chicken ranch, and all the many chicken coops had been remodeled and made into livable dwellings which were homes to many Santa Feans. These were all torn down to make way for pricey condominiums and The Compound became Santa Fe's first gated community.

The restaurant was immediately popular, with good food, drinks and service. Visiting celebrities dined there frequently. One night we spotted the regal-looking Rosalind Russell sitting at a small table in the large rear dining room.

Another time, Marian and I were sitting on a long banco which had a series of tables for two in front of it. It lay against the west wall of the rear dining room and faced a similar, but more booth-like, arrangement on the east wall with free-standing tables lining the center of the room. Gracia Duran and Allen Stamm were sitting at the table next to ours. Gracia turned to me and said, "Look over there at that first booth by the door. The man with his back to us...that's Kirk Douglas!" "Oh, Gracia, it is not. That's Bob Young," I assured her. "I'll bet you," she replied. "Okay, but how are we going to find out?" I challenged. "You go over there and look." "Not on your life, you go!" She obviously was not going to go and, by this time, I was curious. The hair and hint of a beard were about all I could see, and that convinced me it was Bob, so I got up and walked over behind him, put my arm around his shoulder and said, "Hello, Bob." This guy flew out of his chair and stood at his full height, about 5'2". With steely, piercing blue eyes, he stared straight through me as he demanded, "Who is Bob?" I did not falter. I replied cooly, "Bob Young, he owns the bistro, El Farol, and you certainly are not Bob!" I turned and walked back to my table, leaving his wife, who was sitting opposite him, convulsed with suppressed laughter. As I approached my table, I looked at Gracia and said, "You win."

In 1972, another restaurant opened that had a dress code of a different sort. Owned by Willie and June Ortiz, LaTertulia served superb New Mexican food and the best margaritas. Willie was of Spanish ancestry, but June was from the South—Tennessee, I think. However, with her jet black hair, which was piled up on her head and spiked with a jeweled Spanish comb, and piercing black eyes, she looked more Spanish than most of the Spanish ladies in Santa Fe. The restaurant was housed in an adobe building that had at one time been a convent and so had many small to medium dining rooms. June had very rigid, unbreakable rules regarding children and appropriate dress. Because La Tertulia catered to families, as did most restaurants that served New Mexican food, it was frequented by children of all ages. Small children and babies were allowed service in one dining room only. When it was full, that was it! Parents with small fry had to wait or go elsewhere no matter how many vacant tables were to be had in the other dining rooms. No tank tops, shorts or bare feet were allowed, and children less than twelve years old were not allowed on the enchanting outdoor patio and garden. It had been June's observation that children younger than twelve were apt to be restless and run around the patio, and she did not want her other guests disturbed.

One July 4, my cousin, Mike, his wife, Marilyn, and their nine-year-old daughter were visiting for the day, and we wanted to take them to LaTertulia for lunch on the Patio! Knowing June's prohibition, Marian and I both boldly lied about Mackensie's age, swearing she'd be twelve years old in September. June argued with us—stalwart citizens that we were, she was challenging our veracity. "Doesn't look twelve to me," she grumbled as she finally grabbed a hand full of menus and led us to a table on the patio. I understood what June meant when, after we'd been sitting at the table a few minutes, Mackensie began to fidget and wanted to go look at the flowers on the other side of the patio. I gritted my teeth and thought—"If I have to sit on that child, she's not going to get out of that chair." Fortunately, her mother restrained her.

    The oldest restaurant in town, The Pink Adobe, where I had dined during my first visit to Santa Fe, for many years did not have a liquor license, so we had to brown bag it. This was awkward, but the food was exceptional and the atmosphere the most picturesque in a very picturesque town, so it thrived. As more restaurants with liquor licenses began opening in Santa Fe, Rosalea Murphy, the proprietor, faced with more and stiffer competition, finally purchased a liquor license. These licenses were a very precious commodity in Santa Fe, not easy to come by and cost dearly, but it proved to be the right decision. She soon added a new, larger dining room which took a big chunk out of her small parking lot; then, where the outdoor patio had been, a bar and more dining space were added.

    Santa Feans were very protective of their trees, and it was not especially unusual to see a tree sprouting through someone's roof. The tree had been in the way when the house was built and, rather than chop it down, the builder had incorporated it into the interior decor and built the roof around it.

    There were several old trees, left from what had been the outdoor patio, growing happily in Rosalea's new bar. I'm sure it made interesting viewing to unsuspecting tourists not used to such sights to look up from the sidewalk outside and see huge trees erupting through the cantilevered roof.

    Santa Fe's younger set and not-so-younger set made the bar a 5 o'clock hang-out. It became a very in-place.

Rosalea was a sexy, gypsyish-looking woman, very attractive to men. She was married to Ray Murphy and, when he died, she was devastated. She devoted herself to her business and her polo team. Polo was a favorite sport in Santa Fe, and several teams competed for oles from the crowds most weekends.

One night, Marian and I were having dinner at the Pink Adobe for the purpose of taking dining-out photos for that column in *The Santa Fean*. Marian was the photographer, and she left the table in search of lively subjects for her camera. She went into the big dining room and saw Priscilla Hoback (Rosalea's daughter) sitting in the back of the room with a group of guests. Marian approached Priscilla and asked if she could take a photo for the magazine. Horrified, Priscilla said, "Absolutely not!" Marian, bewildered and hurt, crept back to the table and told me. I said, "That's very unlike Priscilla. Let me go take a look." I immediately understood Priscilla's refusal and went back to the table to tell Marian. I should mention that, although Marian always voted, she was apolitical and paid no attention to that part of life. I said, "Marian, the reason Priscilla didn't want her picture taken is because that big, bearded fellow sitting at the table is John Ehrlichman." She looked at me, her vivid blue eyes puzzled. "Who's John Ehrlichman?"

Ehrlichman stayed in Santa Fe for several years. The notoriety wore off, the beard came off, and he became an ordinary Santa Fean.

By this time, the early seventies, Claude had lost interest in cooking and closed the kitchen. She had other interests that she wished to pursue, and we suspected they were the two-legged kind.

To fund her new interests, her hand was always in the till. Even though the place was hers, it's not considered good business practice to steal from oneself. Considering everything, it's no wonder Claude's began a downhill tumble. It hit bottom without a whimper because by then the crowds already had moved elsewhere.

12

Some changes were acceptable to Santa Feans; others were not. When a proposal by the local or state government or any other entity was not to our liking, we went into action, either loudly protesting, quietly sabotaging, or both.

We treasured our dirt roads and actually looked down on those unfortunates who lived on paved streets. Sometime in the 1960s, when the city decided to pave Camino del Monte Sol, it created such furor—not just from residents of the road, but from the whole town—that it made the city quake; however, the contract had been let and the engineers began to lay the curbs. It was a very narrow road and the idea of its being hemmed in by curbs was outrageous—so outrageous, in fact, that Aristide Mian, a sculptor, went out on a dark night and chopped up the curb in front of his house. The next day it was replaced. That night Aristide, who now had the aid of several other artists living along the road, chopped his portion of curb, as did each of the other artists. This continued for several nights with each night bringing more residents into the fray. Then each day the curbs would be replaced. Finally, the contractor gave up and the road was paved without curbs.

When Fluoride was to be added to Santa Fe's water, there were screamers on both sides. Some roared, "Save our children's teeth!"—while purists and Christian Scientists ranted, "Save us from forced medication!" Those for fluoridation won the day, and the children's teeth were saved.

Outrage best describes Santa Feans reaction to Mayor Leo Murphy's and the City Council's decision in 1960 to demolish the Nusbaum house on Washington Avenue to make way for a parking lot. The graceful, 100-year-old house had been built by a merchant, Solomon Spiegelberg, in the 1850's. Built of adobe bricks, the ground floor walls were 2 3/4 feet thick, and the walls of the second story were 1 3/4 feet thick. The 78 foot facade had deep lower and upper portales, tapered square columns supporting the roof overhangs, and pedimented windows.

Irate citizens stormed the local government in its chambers, demanded the stony-faced group, then begged them to save the Nusbaum house from demolition. The uncaring response was "If you want to save it, you'll have to buy it!" The Santa Feans in their fervor, so sure that they could make a difference, left downhearted and defeated.

The city built its parking lot, but the coup de grace was that they also built a bomb shelter underneath it to house only the Mayor and City Council in case of attack.

State government became such big business that, by the early 1960's, it had outgrown its capitol building, and the legislature in 1963 approved funds of more than four and one-half million dollars for construction of a new one. The building, finished in 1966, is built in the shape of the Zia Pueblo Indians' symbol for Sun Father. Round with four short abutments at 6, 9, 12 and 3 o'clock, representing the sun's rays, the capitol's four levels are built around a 60 foot high rotunda with circular glass panels at the top admitting light which focuses on the Great Seal of the State of New Mexico embedded into the rotunda floor below.

The structure resembled a gigantic bull fight arena and was immediately nicknamed "the bull ring." Angry citizens roared their disapproval and created such hullabaloo that the local newspaper ran a picture of the "ring" in its early stages of construction, announcing a forthcoming struggle between Christians and lions.

Clay Buchannan, the head of the grounds' keepers, had planted a virtual forest of trees and shrubs all around the building in an effort to conceal its offensiveness.

Today, the grumblings have ceased and, although some even speak of the unique capitol with a shade of pride, the name "the bull ring" lingers on.

The biggest fight of all occurred over the demise of the Santa Fe National Bank building and its parking lot. A Texas developer had purchased the property and was proposing to build an enormous three-story cement and steel edifice that would fill the whole block from Washington Avenue west to Lincoln. A miniature of the building was presented to the Santa Fe Styles Committee and the City Council. The only concession to Santa Fe style the developer had made was to plaster the exterior an adobe color. It was too bulky, with no set-backs and windows that were too large, too many and incorrectly placed.

The Styles Committee and City Council sold out to the developer who had threatened to build away from downtown if his plans were not approved. Immediately dubbed the "ugly building," it became a subject of ridicule and the brunt of jokes, but it persevered. Today, the trees in front have filled out and softened the facade somewhat, but most of us still turn our heads away when we're in the neighborhood. I think it hurt the bank. Some people were so irate that they took their accounts elsewhere.

13

On September 16, 1712, the Santa Fe Municipal Council, under the auspices of the Governor and Captain General of New Spain in Mexico City, issued a proclamation heralding an annual Fiesta to honor the re-conquest of Santa Fe the latter part of the 17th Century by General Don Diego deVargas from the Indian revolt which had ended victoriously for the Indians in 1682. The Indians occupied the town and its environs until General deVargas, without further bloodshed, retook Santa Fe in 1693.

Fiesta was held sporadically through the early years, then not at all until it was revived in the 1920's. In 1926, John Sloan, the famous painter, his wife, Dolly, and poet, Witter Bynner, were the guiding lights in originating the Hysterical Parade which today is combined with the Historical Parade. Even during the great depression, Fiesta persisted. One year, workers of the local laundry were featured in a float wearing white and carrying placards spoofing the government's alphabet—the C.C.C., N.R.A., W.P.A. and so forth. The owner of the laundry was dressed in shorts, socks and wore a barrel over his torso. And there were always, and still are, Mariachi bands. Fiesta gave way during World War II, but began again with great fervor when it ended.

After the War and well into the 1970's, Fiesta costumes were essential. Perennial favorites for men were the tight-fitting Mexican Charro outfits; braided trousers, bolero jackets, ruffled shirts and wide-brimmed braided hats, or snappy black Flamenco suits worn with high-heeled black boots and sinister, flat-crowned black hats. Easier to come by was the Mexican wedding shirt worn by both men and women with black trousers or white Mexican peon pants.

Velveteen Navajo shirts decorated with silver buttons at the V-neck and at the collar and wrists, worn over trousers for men or full squaw skirts for women, were worn on the outside and hitched at the waist with silver concho belt or brightly colored woven sash.

By far the most elaborate costumes for women were adapted from the squaw dress. Made in a variety of materials from delicate eyelet, lace and voile to soft, supple velvet, they featured wide-petticoated skirts and blouses with elasticized necks so they could be worn on or off the shoulders. Both skirt and blouse were exuberantly garnished with layers of shining braid, rickrack, or ruffles and lace.

In 1980, Marian and I were roaming the Plaza, looking for a booth that served Navajo mutton stew, when two Fiesta officials approached and congratulated us. They gave us each a ribbon proclaiming us First Place Winners in the costume contest. We were wearing Mexican wedding shirts and jeans, our usual attire, which was significant in that it proved that the era of fancy Fiesta dress had ended.

Held in September, Fiesta is a time of partying and thanksgiving. Officially, it is a three-day celebration, but party-loving Santa Feans can't wait, and private pre-Fiesta parties start as early as mid-August.

We usually had a large outdoor party on our patio and garden in August, with as many as 100 diversified guests. That was typical of Santa Fe—you'd see bankers, clerks, artists, hairdressers, civic leaders and do-gooders, musicians, opera singers, doctors, writers, gallery owners, lawyers, restauranteurs, hoteliers, politicos, and half the gays in town mixing and enjoying each other. When you were introduced to someone whom you did not know, it was usually by first names only and you never asked them what they did for a living. That was just not important. I've known people for years without knowing their last names or what, if anything, they did.

One of our favorite guests was an attractive red-head whom we had met when she was entertaining at Rancho de Chimayo, a restaurant of some repute in the Village of Chimayo. She sang and played the guitar, and we always tipped her generously. We didn't know at the time that she was the wife of John McCarty, the Vice President of Frito-Lay, and that this was her hobby. Jackie was charming and intelligent, and had been a teacher in Taos before she married John. Their home, atop a rise among the foothills of the Sangre de Cristos, was colorfully decorated with masses of paintings lining its walls. Jackie drove a black English taxicab.

We had Mariachis or sometimes piano players to entertain at these parties and, unasked, Jackie always favored us with a few songs. She dearly loved to sing and was always tracking down old Mexican songs to learn. One time at the restaurant, we had asked her if she knew Hanicio which we thought the most beautiful of all Mexican melodies. She didn't at the time; but the next time we went there, she came to the table and played and sang it for us. In the meantime, she had made a special trip to Mexico to find a Mariachi group that knew it and would teach it to her.

The burning of *Zozobra*, the most spectacular event during Fiesta, kicks off the hoopla. This effigy of old man gloom is burned while it first roars in anger, then emits shrieks and moans its doom. As it burns and groans, a magnificent display of fireworks is released to the delight of the audience and a tumultuous crescendo of shouts, oles and blowing horns.

The burning was held in Fort Marcy Park and, until the early 70's, first arrivals were allowed to drive their cars into the park to view the event from a front row seat. I had a convertible, and we took my mother and friends to the celebration. We were lucky to get a place, centerfield, about four rows back. We all took picnics and a full bar. While waiting, people mulled around, glass in hand—some even carried bottles of champagne and a stack of plastic cups to give relief to thirsty friends who had failed to provide their own. There wasn't a hint of gloom to be found in that park. All was gaiety and *esprit de corps*.

Afterwards, the Sheriff's Posse, Santa Fe's horsey set, led each row of cars out of the park, quickly, efficiently and safely.

The next stop was the Plaza where the Mariachis were in full sway. And Palace Avenue, the street in front of the Palace of the Governors, was already beginning to swing with dancing celebrants. Food booths lined the other three streets surrounding the central square. Hamburgers, tacos, tamales, enchiladas, fresh corn on the cob, Navajo mutton stew and fry bread were among the mouth-watering offerings.

Fiesta wouldn't be Fiesta without a visit to La Fonda. It was jammed to the vigas and we had to shove our way in through the crowds. We inched our way into the bar and spied a kidney-shaped booth that had only two occupants and a toddler in a stroller where there was room for eight. We squeezed in. The couple accepted our presence and we exchanged names. We had just ordered our drinks when his wife excused herself to go to the restroom. The man looked us over and mournfully said, "My wife's a lesbian, you know." To which my mother brightly replied, "Oh, yes, just like Danny Thomas!" This was years before I heard a similar quip made on a television show. I never knew whether my mother was unusually clever or just very naive.

Parades, processions, the crowning of the Queen, and the *Entrada*, which featured Don Diego de Vargas and his entourage in handsome, bright-colored costumes of the era, crowded the calendar Saturday and Sunday. The final event was the Candlelight Procession which formed at the Cathedral following Mass and was led by the Archbishop of the Diocese. Catholics and many of us non-catholics lined up two-by-two, behind the Archbishop and were handed votives in paper cups to shield the flames from breezes and our hands from dripping wax. It was uplifting to take part in the procession which snaked its way through the streets and up to the Cross of the Martyrs which overlooked the town from atop Fort Marcy hill. But it was awe-inspiring to watch the silent marchers and tiny flames winding and bobbing their way to the top of the hill. Afterward, on that somber, reverential note, the party was over.

14

Creative people have always been drawn to Santa Fe. It is a beehive of talented folk—painters, sculptors, wood carvers, weavers, potters, jewelers, musicians, designers, novelists, poets and performers.

Among these are those who love the theatre; there was Derrik Lewis, an actor, noted for his performance as a regular on the Route 66 TV series, who was also a pianist and song-and-dance man par excellence. He was introduced to Santa Fe during the filming of Route 66 and later spent the opera season there. That summer, he fell hard for Santa Fe's charm and decided to settle there and to get involved with the performing arts. It wasn't long until he formed the non-profit Musical Theatre Association and created a dazzling series of musical triumphs. Delving into Santa Fe's ample talent pool, he made stars of locals: Carol Pederson in his production of *Leonard Bernstein: The Man and His Music*; Jo Shawn Davis in tributes to Cole Porter, Jerome Kern and Gershwin; and Salome Martinez whose lovely voice, in tandem with Derrik's own strong baritone, thrilled audiences in such favorites as *Oh, Coward!*, *I Do! I Do!*, and *The Music Man*—and Derik was indeed Santa Fe's own "Music Man." After four hard years of fighting to keep afloat financially and the constant struggle to find suitable space for his performances, Derrik vanished. It wouldn't be until twenty-five years later when, through the untiring effort of Nancy Zeckendorf, who spearheaded the movement to restore, refurbish and remodel the once magnificent Lensic Theatre, that Santa Fe would have a suitable theatre for the performing arts.

Jinx Junkin, another local theatrical entrepreneur, began her foray into show business through Santa Fe's children by founding The Children's Theatre. The children renamed it Jinx's Magic Theatre, and it stood her well when she began producing and directing Broadway musical comedy. From a town burgeoning with talent, she was able to cast such delightful shows as *Oklahoma, The King and I, Fiddler on the Roof, Mame, Gypsy,* and *Oliver!* For Gypsy, she found Claire Stewart Williamson, a cute little blond grandmother with a gigantic voice, to play the Ethel Merman part of Mama Rose. She was a hit; the show was a hit. To do Oliver!, Jinx needed a large group of kids, and I didn't envy her trying to bring order to a bunch of unruly little monsters—but it was no trick for Jinx. Her years with the Children's Theatre gave her the courage to tackle this young mob, and she brought off a production so very spirited and professional that Broadway would have been jealous.

The Santa Fe Community Theatre was home base for another group of talented Santa Feans. The Theatre had had many predecessors through the years known by various similar titles, but the object was always the same—to produce theatre: drama, musicals, comedy and melodrama. This they did with great flair and flavor.

The *piece de resistance* came during Fiesta when the players wrote and performed the annual melodrama which poked fun at local customs, events and, particularly, politicos.

Plots were up-to-the-minute, hilarious take-offs on the goings-on about town, and the action was usually set in territorial days. Jokes were good-natured, albeit sharp and pointed. The villains and villainesses were smart and wicked; the heroes handsome and dull-witted; and the pretty heroines just plain dumb.

For a number of years, Mildred and Paul Rutledge would haul their steam-calliope to the site of the melodrama, and Mildred would play and sing old favorites with gusto. She had a wonderful, bluesy contralto, and we loved to hear her belt out songs.

Between acts, some of the performers and other locals would perform madcap antics during the olios. One year, petite Julia Seton—she stood just four and a half feet tall—sat upon the villain's (Bob Nugent's) lap and sang old-timey songs with him in her clear, high, little-girl voice, captivating the audience. She was in her late 70's at the time.

Julia had come to Santa Fe in 1930 with her husband, the famed naturalist, illustrator and author, Ernest Thompson Seton, when he bought the 2500 acre Sebastian de Vargas land grant a few miles southeast of Santa Fe. Here they established Seton Village and ran the Seton Institute which offered college credits in all manner of Indian lore, arts and crafts. The Village consisted of the Seton home, called the castle, and many cabins and outbuildings.

A story is told that Seton, divorced from his first wife, fell in love with his secretary, Mrs. Julia Moss Buttree, a lively, adorable, little doll of a woman. However, there was a Mr. Buttree which was cause for Seton's consternation. Not to be thwarted, Seton arranged, persuaded or coerced Buttree into divorcing Julia and marrying Seton's cook, Georgia. Buttree was a scrawny, ugly little man with a bulbous nose—a Jimmy Durante without the charm. Georgia was a slim, attractive woman with silvery, prematurely white hair.

After Seton died, the Buttrees opened a restaurant in one of the cabins on the property, called The Silver Mask. It later was moved to a more accessible location on the old Las Vegas Highway and received a small amount of notoriety when it became known that a full-grown bobcat prowled the premises. The Buttrees had discovered the kit abandoned and had raised it to maturity. It was BIG and, though it was more or less domesticated, I would not have turned my back on it.

15

Jacques Cartier, effete and delusional, thought himself a great dancer, somewhat like a Rudolf Nureyev. The only dancing I ever saw him do was his annual ritual to *Zozobra*, where he bobbed, swayed and hopped up and down the steps leading to the big gloom and lit the fuse that would end it all.

He was also a self-proclaimed award-winning designer of Japanese-like gardens. He had designed a terraced lawn for Moya Canning. It was a long, narrow stretch in front of her house which abutted bosum mountain. He created two tiers with a fountain at the end, hand-laid of native stone. He filled the two tiers generously with fresh soil and sodded each. Some years later, it was discovered that he had laid in soil well above the foundation line and into the adobe frame of the house. The constant watering was eroding away the adobe walls.

I will admit that his own extensive gardens were lovely and did look and feel very Japanesey. Composed of small gardens, the extensive landscaping included restful gazebos with comfortable seating spaced here and there between the flowering areas. Big Japanese lanterns lit the way at night between gardens, and faintly tinkling temple bells sang in the light breeze. Vines and flowers nestled amidst large and small boulders with a little waterfall that trickled down to a shallow reflecting pool below. Pea-size gravel formed paths that led from one garden to another, and an irrigation ditch suffused among them. An arched bridge crossed the ditch to join two paths. Shaded by huge trees and flowering bushes, the silence of the tranquil gardens was broken only by wind, water and the twittering of birds.

Jacques lived just beyond Pojoaque in the hills to the East. His house was large and rambling, with room upon room leading one into another as is often the case with old Spanish-built homes. Jacques had married Zena deRossin under protest—Cecily Cunha had discovered the two in compromising circumstances in one of the bedrooms at Rancho Ancon. When Zena found that she was pregnant, Cecily had no illusions about the cause. Cecily was usually like a big, gentle, lumbering bear, but she could make her point when she felt like it. She told Jacques in no uncertain terms that he was going to marry Zena. So Zena and their son, along with Jacques and his friend, Ray, lived together up on the hill—Jacques and Ray in the main house, and Zena and her son in the guest house.

One time, Jacques, in his gardening mode, was driving his station wagon on the highway toward his home in Pojoaque. The back end of the wagon was full to the brim with plants—mostly marigolds—when a siren howled him off to the side of the road. The cops hauled him and his car full of marigolds back to town and, thinking the marigolds were marijuana plants, they cited him for possession. It naturally made the front page of the *New Mexican* and titillated the whole town.

In the summer of 1955, I worked briefly for Paul Ragel who, in addition to owning a popular filling station downtown at the corner of Water Street and Galisteo, had the only car rental agency in town, an Avis franchise. Its office was a little hole-in-the-wall across the street from the side entrance to La Fonda. There was not much call for rentals in those days and, after I'd written dun letters to all of the deadbeats that previous office sitters had neglected, I had plenty of time on my hands.

When I wasn't reading *True Confessions* or one of the large supply of movie magazines—the only reading material to be had, thanks to the taste of Paul's wife, Elida, who sat the office when there was no one else—I stared out the window, fascinated by the never-ending parade of folk passing into and out of La Fonda.

Every day about noon, a big black, chauffer-driven Cadillac would pull up to the door and an attractive, well-dressed middle-aged woman would get out of the car and go into La Fonda. About three hours later, the Cadillac would again appear and wait. Sometimes traffic would force the driver around the block three or four times before the handsome woman would appear, get in the car and be driven away.

I wondered who she was and what she was doing in La Fonda all that time. One day, I caught one of the bell-men outside, asked him about her, and found out that she was a Mrs. Flint from Texas who spent the summers with her daughter, Pauline, in Santa Fe. Every day she had lunch and played bridge at La Fonda.

The Flints had a handsome house off Cerro Gordo, just north of the entrance to the lane leading to my house. I met Pauline on upper Cerro Gordo one afternoon when we were both marooned by turbulent waters, caused by a sudden summer storm in the mountains, gushing down the arroyo which crossed the road. We waited frustrated and impatient for the road to clear.

Pauline was a beautiful young woman, dark-haired, tall and willowy. She later married Rudolf Kieve, our friendly local psychologist/ psychiatrist. Previously, Rudy had been married to Tooky in a tumultuous relationship that local gossips said almost did him in.

I later met Tooky, who had an antique shop on Upper Canyon Road and was remarried to a red-haired piano player named Chavez. Tooky was a slight, dark, mysterious woman—there was something of a sorceress about her, or so it seemed to me. I bought a big black pot— the kind that had been used to render pig fat or that witches use to boil their brew—because I wanted the pot, but also because I felt intimidated not to. I was glad to pay up and get out of that shop.

A sight that never failed to thrill me, as I stared from my window at Avis-Rent-A-Car, was of Greer Garson swooping up the street in her green, open convertible with her flowing red hair flying. Sometimes she would park and go into La Fonda. More often than not, she would have on a handsome riding outfit complete with boots, and sometimes a western hat contained her ample tresses.

She and her husband, Buddy Fogelson, spent summers on their large ranch, Forked Lightening, out by Pecos, about fifteen miles southeast of Santa Fe. I remember seeing her at the Opera, dressed in a dazzling silvery-white gown with a bright scarlet cape competing with her equally bright scarlet locks. What a picture!

Years later, when Greer was coming to Santa Fe from her home in Texas to accept an award from the Santa Fe Festival of the Arts, Marian and I were elected to pick her up at the Albuquerque Airport.

She arrived from the ramp in a wheelchair (which most intelligent women over 50 understand the wisdom of doing) with dark glasses, no makeup and her head uncovered, the famous red hair exposed for all to see. It would have been impossible to miss her in a crowd.

By this time, Greer would have been in her late seventies, yet her skin was smooth and unwrinkled. Of course, the fabulous red hair now came out of a bottle, but she was still a gorgeous woman. She was easy to talk to, and the return trip to Santa Fe passed quickly.

We later received a postcard from her and, on the front, was a picture of her in full western regalia, nuzzling her horse named *Ho Hum Silver*.

Greer and her husband, Buddy, were active ranchers and equally active in the civic affairs of both the village of Pecos and the city of Santa Fe.

Greer bred Santa Gertrudis cattle, not for beef, but for crossbreeding to improve herds of other breeds in this country and abroad.

She bought her bull and his seven brides at the annual auction in Perth, Scotland. Through selective breeding, she was able to produce a pure white herd. Normally, most Scottish Shorthorns are either red or roan.

While Greer bred cattle, Buddy doted on race horses and had a stable of thoroughbreds among which were some winners.

The Fogelsons discovered ancient Pueblo ruins and the ruins of a 16th century mission church on their vast ranch. To preserve them and keep them safe for posterity, they deeded the land and surrounding acreage to the federal government to become the Pecos National Historic Monument.

Greer and Buddy were very generous and gave many awards, scholarships and grants to both individuals and universities. They were especially helpful to the College of Santa Fe, with Greer establishing and funding a theatre center and artist-in-residence program, and Buddy a major grant to fund the college library. With an additional grant of $3 million, Greer also made it possible for the college to develop the Greer Garson Communications Center, a unique state-of-the-art production facility suitable for use by students as well as professionals.

Many movies have been made throughout the years in Santa Fe and around New Mexico. As early as 1912, America's sweetheart, Mary Pickford, played the part of an Indian maiden in the film, *Pueblo Legend*. Tom Mix made a series of films in the Las Vegas area, and Gallup became the focus for a number of westerns made during the 1940's and 50's. Ranches around Santa Fe provided the setting for several movies, but it was the J.W. Eaves Ranch, with its real western town built by J.W. himself, that lured some of the big ones to Santa Fe, including *Where Angels Go, Trouble Follows* starring Rosalind Russell, and *The Cheyenne Social Club* with Jimmy Stewart, Henry Fonda and Shirley Jones.

By far the funniest movie made in the area, at least from my point of view, was *Lust in the Dust*, a spoof of westerns starring Laine Kazan, Tab Hunter and Divine. In one scene, our famous Navajo painter, R.C. Gorman, drew a treasure map on the bare behinds of Laine and Divine, half of the map on each. You can imagine the possibilities this condition would impose.

While they were in town doing the filming, Marian happened to be downtown browsing in a local ladies store, Origins. With a blouse over her arm that she had picked from the rack to try on, she was about to enter one of the dressing rooms when out popped Laine Kazan—in full view of the entire store, naked as a new born babe! Marian was only mildly taken aback, because of her close proximity. No one else even noticed.

16

I never found Santa Feans dull or boring. They were peppy, animated and, above all, individualistic; they also were tellers of absurd tales and prone to engage in outlandish episodes.

For example, there was Winnabelle Beasley: It was a thrilling, terrifying, death-defying ride to take off down Santa Fe's narrow streets in the side-car of a Harley with Winnie at the handlebars. Dressed flamboyantly in tight pants, fringed jacket and boots of matching color, she maneuvered that contraption all over town.

Winnie lived on a horse ranch in the village of Tesuque, a few miles north of the city, where she taught riding and, for a fee, took groups on day-long picnic rides across the hilly, unfenced countryside. Winnie was also a flyer and had earned her commercial license before World War II in Des Moines, Iowa. During the war, she became a member of Jacqueline Cochran's (a famous woman aviator of the time) Air Transport Auxiliary, and flew damaged fighters and huge, injured, four-engine bombers in for repairs from remote places in England, Scotland and Wales. It was while she was in England that she learned to ride a motorcycle and developed a fondness for that mode of transport.

Back at the ranch, Winnie raised four sons, enumerable dogs and multitudinous mice to feed her pet bull-snakes. Her large, beautiful (on the outside) adobe house was bedlam on the inside, full of dogs, escaping mice and prowling snakes.

Musically, Winnie was an accomplished gut-bucket player. This unusual instrument is made by upending a large, galvanized iron wash tub and inserting a broom handle through a hole drilled in its center. The broom handle is then fitted, top to bottom, with a waxed archery bow-string. Winnie was a vigorous and enthusiastic bow-string strummer.

One night, we had had dinner at Shidoni Restaurant, which enjoyed a brief stint of popularity housed in the old Williams Ranch in Tesuque, and went into the bar afterward. There was Winnie in colorful motorcycle garb strumming gaily away on the gut-bucket supported by spirited piano back-up. What fun! But the highlight of the evening came when Crystal Vaughn, who was sitting at a table with her husband and had been ill for some time, rose from her chair, walked over to the two performers and favored us with song after song. She was feeling good that night and I believe that was the last time she ever sang in public. How fortunate we were.

Among my favorite people was Dorothy Wolgamood, an accomplished pianist who taught many Santa Fe youngsters the basics on her colossal concert grand piano that she had purchased and had shipped from Vienna, Austria. Dorothy also made brilliantly colorful, amusing collages. Marian and I owned three of them. And with her near perfect figure, Dorothy was much in demand to model clothes which she did mostly for Suzette's, one of our local up-scale boutiques. She also frequented The Palace bar where oft times we would see her. She always greeted us with a happy smile and a witty comment in her tiny, high-pitched, bell-like voice.

Dorothy and her husband, Leo, moved to Santa Fe from Colorado where Leo had earned his architectural degree. Leo went to work for John Gaw Meem whom many credit with being the father of

Santa Fe style as we know it. The pair bought the old Applegate house on El Caminito, a little lane off Camino del Monte Sol. Because there were no street lights on either El Caminito or the Camino, they carried a lantern to light their way of an evening to Roybal's Bar on Canyon Road. Dorothy told a story about coming home from the bar one night just a wee bit tiddly. The light from their swaying lantern picked up a long bundle of rags in the road. Dorothy, incensed at the mess on her road, gave it a swift kick. The bundle grunted and an apparition half rose up. Dorothy screamed, terrified. "Leo, what is it? It made a noise and moved. It must be that ghost from the house we were warned about!" She was near hysterics. Leo, who had gone over to investigate, gave the bundle another kick. This time there was an audible, very angry "ouch!" And the creature rose up, arms and legs flaying, and yelled. "Whacha mean kickin a man in 'ish bed. Get outta 'ere!" Dorothy laughed at the telling and noted, "He was a lot drunker than we were so we decided to let him be; but we saw him many times after that, sound asleep in the middle of the dirt road. Leo decided that the dirt held the warmth from the sun for a long time, so the road made a cozy resting place."

Concha Ortiz y Pino de Kleven came from a long line of Pinos and Ortizes home-based in the small village of Galisteo about 20 miles south of Santa Fe. Her family owned an enormous ranch of many thousand acres and, when her father died, she ran the ranch single-handedly for a time. Concha, strong-willed, was always heavily involved in good works, civic affairs and politics. Bright and demanding, she could cut a person down with a look if anyone was dumb enough to oppose one of her pet projects.

Concha, although petite in stature, had a presence ten feet tall. She was a handsome woman with a strong, prominent nose and always wore her thick dark hair wrapped in a circular bun high around her head. She loved to explain the reason for the hairdo. "Mother," she would begin, "thought my nose too large and took me to New York to find out if something could be done about it. She took me to several plastic surgeons for evaluation with unsatisfactory results so, in despair, she said to me, 'At least we can get something done about your hair while we're here.' Off to a hair stylist we went. The stylist was confident and considerate and listened patiently to my mother bemoan my lack of a nose job because of the incompetent plastic surgeons we had been to see. He listened and then began whipping my hair around this big doughnut thing. 'Now, Madam, look!' he instructed my mother. 'You see the hairdo detracts and your daughter's nose retreats and she no longer needs a nose job.' Mother was simply ecstatic and never tired of singing his praises, and I've worn my hair the same way ever since."

In her youth, Concha won election to the New Mexico House of Representatives and became the only woman in the United States to become the Whip of the majority party.

We were on several boards together and saw each other at parties and other gatherings. Concha, her sister, Mela, and her brother-in-law came to our house every Christmas day after mass for a glass of sherry.

Concha hated use of the word *Hispanic* because she said, "It is about as accurate a description of national heritage or ethnic background as the word Anglo. Hispanic lumps all Spanish-speaking peoples and even some Portuguese into one big catchall without consideration for the great diversification in cultures among Spaniards, Cubans, Brazilians, Argentines, Ecuadorians, Peruvians, Costa Ricans and Mexicans, to name a few. It is as much a misnomer as it is that many of the local Spanish call everyone that isn't of Spanish ancestry Anglo. I was having tea at a friend's home one afternoon and, when her young son came home from school, I asked him, 'Manuel, how is school this year?' He replied politely, 'It's just fine, Senora. We have only one Anglo and he's a Negro!'"

I haven't seen Concha in a while. She must be well into her nineties now, but I expect she still has her hand in something.

Frank Ortiz y Davis was related to Concha. I think he was her cousin, but he may have been her brother. Traditional Spanish families honored their ancestors by using the surnames of both parents, father's name first. Hence Ortiz y Pino means the father was Ortiz and the mother a Pino, whereas Ortiz y Davis would indicate that the father was again Ortiz, but the mother was a Davis. Concha's and Frank's fathers may have been brothers which would make them cousins and explain the difference in their mothers' maiden names.

Frank owned a bar and a museum that sat alongside the highway into Galisteo. He also owned a huge spread on which he raised beef cattle. We spent many happy hours chatting with Frank in his bar and browsing in his cluttered, dusty museum. He was a garrulous old rapscallion and told us many tall tales which we enjoyed without necessarily believing.

There was a large pueblo ruin on his property where we liked to go hunting potsherds. The pasture abutted the highway for miles and was fenced in with barbed-wire. We were old hands at outwitting barbed-wire fences so this presented no deterrent when we wanted to got pot hunting. The ruin lay about a mile into the property off the highway. One day we were driving in the area and had our two dogs in the back of the station wagon when we decided we'd stop to see what we could find in the ruin and give the dogs a good run. They got a good run alright! We had both been busy, eyes downcast, searching for sherds or whatever else of interest we might find, when Marian looked up and around and said, "Where are the dogs?" I glanced up, concerned, and searched this way and that. They were nowhere in sight. More than a little panicky, we raced up the nearest rise and finally spotted them way off in the distance. They were having the time of their lives, barking and racing after Frank's whole herd of cattle. I groaned in dismay. "Oh, Lord, Marian, they're running pounds off those steers! If Frank comes along and sees this, we're in for big trouble!" We whistled, called, pleaded and cajoled our wayward pets. They finally heard us and, wonder of wonders, responded. They must have sensed the terror in our voices. The four of us raced across the meadow, through the barbed-wire, over the asphalt and into our car parked at the side of the road. I had just pulled out onto the highway when I glanced in the rear-view mirror and there was Frank's old truck lumbering along behind us. Whew! That one was a little too close, but we made it.

17

A thriving wood yard occupies a sprawling acre or more on one of Santa Fe's most sought-after and expensive residential streets, Camino del Monte Sol. Jesus Rios, founder of the legendary Rios Wood Yard, bought the Camino del Monte Sol property in the 1930s. He began adding rooms on to the two-room adobe that was there until he had nine rooms, enough to accommodate him, his wife, Teresa, and their eight children, as well as the office of the wood yard.

Rios had been born in Old Mexico and brought to New Mexico by his parents when he was a wee tot. Always an early riser and a hard worker, he began earning his livelihood when he was big enough to heft a shovel.

As his sons grew, he imbued in them his work ethic which was simply—"get up early, eat and get to work."

His business grew with his sons. They were not only supplying firewood to most of Northern New Mexico, but also fence posts, vigas (ceiling beams in the round), coyote fencing (slim cedar posts placed upright, wired together, braced midway top and bottom with horizontal posts) and latillas (young, narrow, peeled aspen limbs set side by side or in a herringbone pattern between vigas to form the ceiling).

Most everyone bought their firewood from Rios' because you could depend on the quality—it would be the much sought-after piñon and not cedar mixed with cottonwood.

Mrs. Rios, the dragon-lady, manned the telephone and it was wise to stay on her good side because, if you were demanding or the slightest bit discourteous, you could wait 'til hell froze over for your wood to be delivered.

Jesus himself usually came with one of his sons, Juan, to deliver the wood. We always called him "Mr. Rios," but his sons by their given names. They stacked the wood methodically—each layer cross-hatching the preceding one. I once asked him, "How did you get your sons to lay the wood so exactly?" Proudly, he replied, "When they were young I taught them how to stack the wood just so and when they didn't do it right, they had to do it again and again, until it was perfect."

As the years went by, the property containing the wood yard became increasingly more precious. I said something to Jesus about this one day and he said, "Yes, I know about my property. Why just the other day some crazy gringo offered me a million dollars for it. I laughed and told him, 'And, Mr. Million Dollars, what would I do with my wood yard if I sold you my property?'"

Jesus Rios was born in 1900 and died in his mid-nineties. But Juan and the other sons carry on the business and the wood yard is still at that million dollar address on Camino de Monte Sol.

Elita Wilson was a social climber in a city where the ladder was horizontal rather than vertical. Lofty and opportunistic, Elita was also a name-dropper in a place where names had no meaning. Although she was outspoken and caustic, beneath the vitriolic exterior lay a tough resiliency.

Never one to hide behind false modesty, Elita loved to crow about her exploits. She was multi-talented and had used those talents advantageously. She was athletic and, in her youth, had been a gold-medal swimmer, an expert trap-shooter and a darn good golfer. She was a gifted pianist. She had sung and danced in a traveling vaudeville show and had acted in several New York Broadway plays. Elita was an able writer and had authored several books and copious magazine articles and stories. She said of her writing, "I was a prolific, financially-successful hack."

During World War II, she took up photography and studied at a New York school where she was an apt pupil. She became a photographer of note, specializing in portraits of adults, children and pets.

After the war, Elita, quite worn out from her hectic New York life, visited a guest ranch outside Santa Fe to recuperate. She became so taken with the area that she decided to stay. She met Boo Emmet, a remittance woman from the East, and together they opened a small specialty shop in Tesuque. Elita designed and had made elegant Fiesta wear and other Southwestern attire. Her clothes were so in demand that she closed her small Tesuque shop and opened a larger boutique in the city.

In the meantime, Elita met Major Felton, an art-deco painter and illustrator. Although she knew he was married, she set her cap for him anyway. She succeeded! Major, bewitched, divorced his wife and married Elita.

Boo, her former partner, was so entranced that, completely under Elita's spell, she faithfully ran errands and did whatever else Elita bade her to do until the day she died.

After Major died, Elita, always at her best in the face of adversity, went to work selling art for Jamison's Galleries and became a top-notch sales person, sought after by competing galleries. When I commented to her, "Elita, I didn't know you knew so much about art," she retorted in her own inimical style, "My dear, of course, I know all about art!"

That was Elita. She knew all about anything that she needed to know to tackle whatever life dealt.

Chuck Barrows, penniless, hitchhiked, walked and hopped freight cars to get to Santa Fe from New York in 1928. He was not very tall, sort of stubby, but muscular with a burly torso. By the time I knew him, his hair was mostly white and worn combed forward with straight evenly-cut bangs across his brow. He had a strong, pleasing face, and his eyes sparkled with deviltry.

Chuck was an artist and a mycologist of note. He had discovered numerous new varieties of fungi which he documented meticulously by painting their images in habitat, making spore prints and describing the taste, color and effect, if any, of each.

His wife, Mary, worried about him some because he was his own guinea pig, tasting and even eating the hitherto unknown types of mushrooms he found. She did admit that sometimes Chuck's reaction to eating a strange fungus was so ludicrous that she had to laugh— like the time one afternoon when he brought home one that made him so thirsty that he drank two gallons of iced tea and, swollen like a blow fish, he began to laugh and laugh and laugh. She wiped her eyes from laughing at the memory and said, "He didn't stop laughing until midnight. But there was one time when we thought we were going to lose him. He developed a high fever, his face and torso turned bright red and he began raving unintelligibly. It was like someone speaking in tongues, but much worse. Fortunately, a friend of ours was a house guest and, together, we got him in the bath tub filled with cold water to which we added as much ice as we could find. We'd take turns rubbing ice over his head and at his temples and, finally, after hours, he began to calm down and then his temperature suddenly plummeted and he was back to normal."

Those events didn't deter Chuck. He was always ready for more adventure. He was also a mischievous rascal and enjoyed shocking others with his antics.

I remember seeing him at an Artists' Ball one year. The theme was "Aliens from Mars" and Chuck went all out. He sprayed his hair, face, arms, legs and torso with green paint and wrapped a white knee-length sarong around his waist. During one of the dances, a bunch of the revelers were doing crazy stunts—waving their arms up and down, bending at the waist with arms stretched toward the floor, and some even bending clear over to walk four-footed with palms on the floor as forelegs and their backsides high in the air—all this time circling the dance floor. And among these, there was Chuck, sans undergarment, with his privates painted green and exposed for all to see!

"A lot of people think I'm an elevator, but I'm not!" was an oft-quoted comment made by Emily Otis Barnes. Her father, Joseph E. Otis, was a Chicago banker and director of the Santa Fe Railroad. Emily grew up in Chicago but, during her youth, visited the Southwest and Santa Fe many times. She married Nathaniel Owens of Skidmore, Owens and Merrill, of architectural firm fame; and the couple produced four children. Shortly after World War II ended in 1946, they bought a 40-acre ranch in Pojoaque, New Mexico, and lived there for a number of years until their divorce in 1953. Emily was married briefly to an Albuquerque artist whose last name was Barnes, but his first name escapes me. When they broke up, Emily lived in New York City for about 15 years. She returned to live in Santa Fe about 1970, which was when I met her.

Emily appeared to be an aristocratic, aloof sort but, on further appraisal, her smiling eyes and laugh lines turning up at the corners of her mouth seemed to refute her appearance. Knowing Emily was to realize in the tall, slim woman a bubbly, jubilant personality full of fun and quick wit. For many years, we were neighbors and were frequently together. She lived in an old house exuberant with color—reds, oranges and yellows—mixed with handsome, aged Navajo rug wall-hangings, Indian pottery and modernly-styled furniture.

She would entertain us with her "drunken-chicken" dinners (her own recipe, the ingredients of which were not divulged), and we would take her to dinner when we were going out to shoot photos for the dining-out column in *The Santa Fean Magazine*. One time, when we were at a New Mexican restaurant having beers with our spicy dinners, she picked up two of the bottle caps which had double X's on their surfaces. She poked them in her eyes and insisted Marian take her picture, which she did, and we ran it in the magazine, much to the astonished amusement of our subscribers.

Emily wasn't all nonsense. She had deep ties to Santa Fe from her youth and fiercely strove to protect its culture. She served on the Board of the Old Santa Fe Association and on the Historical Design Review Board. She had many Indian friends and worked untiringly in their behalf. She often said, "If there are other lives, I'm sure I was once an Indian." From 1971 to 1975, Emily was Executive Secretary of the Southwestern Association on Indian Affairs which oversees Santa Fe's annual Indian Market. Later, she served on the Board of the Wheelwright Museum of the American Indians and, in 1983, she became President of that august body.

Emily contributed much to Santa Fe and to the lives of all the people who knew her. She was in her 90s when she died in the 1990s.

Alice Rossin (Mrs. Edgar) came to Santa Fe in 1916 with her famous parents. Her father, William Penhallow Henderson, was an eminent painter and her mother, Alice Corbin Henderson, a noted poet and associate editor of *Poetry Magazine*. Alice was about ten years old at the time and, according to her own accounts, a nosey brat.

The family lived on Camino del Monte Sol and "little" Alice immediately immersed herself into her neighbors' lives. She said that she quickly learned Spanish, her neighbors' language, so that she'd be better able to help them solve their problems. She confessed that she often stepped in between a battling husband and wife, told an unmarried mother that she should have a husband, and advised them all on the correct way to raise their children. She was not yet eleven years old. She also admitted that she took up smoking cigarettes and even experimented with chewing tobacco.

Alice rode horseback all over town and, when she had time, attended school at Loretto Academy for a while. But she was too high-spirited for the sisters, so she was tutored in succession by three different young women, each of short duration. Finally, the youngest and last of the three to teach Alice announced to Alice's mother that educating "little" Alice was hopeless. This delighted "little" Alice and gave her more time for her other activities.

When she was fifteen years old, Alice married John Evans, the only child of Mabel Dodge Luhan of Taos. She and John lived in New York City where she had three daughters by the time she was nineteen. I don't know whether John died or they were divorced but, at the age of twenty-five, she became a single mother and returned to Santa Fe with her three daughters.

To support them, Alice opened a shop in Tesuque where she sold Indian pots, rugs and jewelry, as well as women's clothing of her own designs. She designed bandana dresses and casual outfits made of denim which became so popular that she opened additional shops in Tucson and Chandler, Arizona.

She chuckled when she told me about what she considered to be her biggest coup. "Best and Company in New York bought my dresses for sale in the New York store, and I still have a copy of one of their ads which appeared in the New York Sun announcing my bandana dresses."

When Alice was in New York on one of her buying trips, she met Edgar Rossin, whom she later married. They lived in New York and London for a number of years but, when he died, Alice moved back in the late 1960s to Santa Fe and settled on her ranch in Tesuque.

I met Alice in the mid-1970s when she was about 70 years old. She came by her name "little" honestly for she was tiny, attractive, with dark, flashing eyes. She was sharp, quick and astute.

By this time, she owned El Nido, the popular roadside restaurant in Tesuque. The El Nido property butted her ranch property. I don't know how she came to own it, but suspect she bought it for a song after Ray Arias was killed in a traffic accident. Ray and Irene had purchased El Nido from Charlie and Mimi Besre and had run it successfully. But after Ray was killed, the rumor was that Irene and her son, Steve, were having a hard time.

Alice and a friend of hers tried their hands running it for a while, but restaurants are hard work and require constant attention. So Alice bought out her partner and hired a manager, Carlton Colquit. Carlton was a young man in his mid-forties and good-looking.

We discovered they had become an item when, upon being invited to our annual Fiesta party, Alice asked if she could bring Carlton. It wasn't very long after our party that the phone rang about 10:30 one night. I answered, groggy with sleep, and it was "little' Alice. She said gaily, "We wanted you and Marian to know that we just got married!" "What?" I yelled into the phone, "Who is the other half of we?" "Why, Carlton, of course, dear," she replied sweetly. Dazed and still a little groggy, I roared, "What did you do that for?" Immediately I thought, "What a thing for me to say!" But she assured me, " Because we wanted to."

I found out the real reason much later. Two of Alice's three daughters had long since died, and Alice was not especially fond of the one remaining. Alice had found out that she had terminal cancer and, because Carlton had been her constant companion and very kind and helpful to her, she wanted to leave her estate to him. Knowing how grasping her daughter was and that she would battle to get what she believed to be rightfully hers, Alice shrewdly covered her tracks. She not only married Carlton, she had made an iron-clad will with Santa Fe's most reputable lawyers and had it witnessed by citizens of impeccable character. Alice, certain that her daughter would contest the will anyway, went a step further and had herself examined by two psychiatrists. Their written reports attesting to her sanity and continued ability to make her own decisions were attached to the will. After Alice died, her daughter did contest the will, resulting in a drawn-out and messy process. The daughter's lawyers tried to prove that Carlton was gay. What that would have accomplished, I don't know. Because Marian and I had known them both well, one of the investigators came to question us. Among other questions, he asked, "Is Carlton gay?" We both answered, "How do you think we would know that?" But the question that took the prize was, "Was the marriage consummated?"

My eyebrows shot up and Marian's mouth dropped open, speechless. I gathered my wits about me and replied, "I can't believe you asked that question, and you surely don't expect an answer. Not any people that I know or have ever known volunteer those intimate details to their friends, and I believe you've asked your last question of us."

In spite of all the brouhaha, Alice's foresight and craftiness triumphed and Carlton won the case.

R C. Gorman, Navajo painter, refused to say what the initials stood for. He loved to tease and he'd tell a serious Texan, "R.C. stands for Rosemary Clooney, but I don't sing so well." One time in one of the galleries representing his work, he replied to a browser who was interested in one of his paintings but demanded to know his name, "Well, sir, it's Reginald Chauncy, but I don't want people to know it because, with a name like that, you have to be a good fighter, and I'm a lover not a fighter." He was so gleeful over that comeback he could barely keep a straight face in the telling.

R.C. was born in Chinle, Arizona and grew up in that remote, starkly-beautiful land. His father, Carl, one of the famous Navajo code-talkers during World War II, was also an artist of note but never received the international recognition that has been granted to his son. R.C. spent most of his formative years among women, particularly his mother, an aunt and his grandmother, because the men were all away at war. This may be one of the reasons why he became entranced with female grace and beauty and why women have been the inspiration and models for all his paintings.

Although R.C. lives in Taos, he has been a regular visitor to Santa Fe. We'd see him at The Palace Restaurant dressed in his usual flamboyant Hawaiian shirt and brightly colored headband. At one meeting, I asked him how the building of his new house was going. "It's all finished," be beamed, "and I've already had it blessed by a Navajo medicine man and a Catholic priest, and I'm looking for the right rabbi to do the same thing. I don't take any chances!" he chuckled.

R.C., always playful and good natured, loves people, beautiful things, good food, his hundreds of headbands and Hawaiian shirts. I asked him once where he got all his headbands and shirts. "Oh, my headbands come from my many admirers—all women, naturally," he winked and grinned, "and my shirts are custom made for me by Harriet's of Honolulu. Every time I go over there I order more shirts and each time we go one size larger!" he chortled.

We met Chris Griscom years before she became THE New Age Guru. It was the winter of 1973 and she had dug a grow-hole in her yard in Galisteo in which she was growing fresh vegetables and herbs. Although a thick layer of snow covered the ground above, the grow-hole, six feet or so in the earth and covered with plastic, was surprisingly warm.

I don't know just when or how Chris got religion, but Shirley MacLaine found her at the Light Institute of Galisteo and was counseled by her in the intricacies of New Age theory. Later, the actress wrote a best-selling book, *Dancing in the Light,* about her experience. The popularity of the book put Chris and Sante Fe in the limelight and undoubtedly contributed to Santa Fe's allure for crowds of crystal healers, channelers, psychics and body workers. Santa Fe became a New Age capital for all those seeking enlightenment.

Although Chris was a dark-haired, healthy-looking young woman when we met her, she became very ethereal in appearance with long, straight blond hair which I'm sure added to her mystique.

She has become internationally famous, spreading her spiritual message around the world, and is an author of many books on the subject. She received further widespread fame when her sixth child was born in the warm waters off the coast in the Bahamas.

Thus Chris Griscom and all the rest, as well as many others, have made their special contributions to the life and times of the nearly half century that I lived in Santa Fe.

18

Indians are ubiquitous to Santa Fe. Every day they sit on their blankets under the portal of the Palace of the Governors selling their jewelry. Only Indians, by special dispensation of the Museum authorities, can sell their wares under the portal. Other vendors are relegated to the block across the street and, chosen in a lottery system, are licensed by the city.

There are many Indian painters and sculptors so they frequented gallery openings as well as private parties around town.

There are still nineteen inhabited pueblos in New Mexico and six of them lie within 30 miles of Santa Fe. Santo Domingo is the largest of these pueblos and, being ultra conservative, is very strict about the behavior of its residents and its visitors. You don't dare get out of line while at that pueblo because, if you do, you will be faced with severe consequences.

Almost every year, Marian and I went to Santo Domingo to the great Tablita Dance commonly called the Corn Dance held August 4.

Open to the public, it was a very popular event. Because it attracted visitors from all over the world, it was crowded and parking was a nightmare. We managed to squeeze the car into a small space fairly close to the Pueblo and the dance plaza. Since it was a hot summer day, we were both dressed in white blouses and white jeans to defray the sun's rays. We found a place in front on the ground at the edge of the dance area almost under an overhanging portal.

Shortly after we had found our seats, a bugler standing in front of the church blew a loud triumphant command on his horn; the drummers stationed to one side of the dance plaza beat a roll on their drums; and two officials standing atop the Kivas shot their guns in the air. Male Indians erupted from the church carrying the image of their patron saint and, with the priest leading, walked to a green bower made from leafy cottonwoods set up at one end of the plaza. The saint was left inside the bower to be guarded by musket-toting elders. Women of the village had left offerings of bread, chile stew and fruit. Now that all is in order, the dance begins.

It is a sacred religious ritual that is a prayer for rain and fertile fields. First come the zebra-painted Koshares, sacred clowns who race though the pueblo shouting a summons to the dancers. The Koshares perform silly antics and stunts, but also keep the crowds settled and under control and, when needed, attend to dancers who are having difficulty with their dress.

There are two kivas in the pueblo—the turquoise and the squash—and each sends forth a plethora of dancers who perform in separate, alternating groups.

The large group of drummers is reinforced by a chorus of as many as sixty men and boys whose deep, rich voices, combined with the steady rumble of the drums, provide the background for each group of dancers who stream down the kiva steps and form into lines with the men and women facing each other.

The men wear Hopi-made, hand-woven white kilts decorated with red, green and black designs. The kilts are bound at the waist with a bright red sash with fox tails hanging down the rear. They wear a band of rattles behind each knee and carry a sprig of evergreen in one hand and a gourd rattle in the other.

The women are barefoot and clad in black mantas embroidered in red and green which fasten over one shoulder, leaving the other bare. Around their waists are red decorated sashes similar to those worn by the men. On their heads they wear tablitas which are thin boards cut in the shape of an altar, painted blue with bits of feathers stuck to the tips. They also carry evergreen boughs.

The men dance, heads held high and tilted slightly back, with spirited high stamping steps. They shake their rattles in unison with the drum beat. The women dance with eyes downcast while their feet move in little shuffling steps.

Sitting cross-legged on the ground, we could feel the earth throb with the drum beat and dancing feet.

When one group finished its dance, another group began, but not necessarily right away. It's Indian time and the next dance will begin when "the time is right"—which may be minutes or an hour.

We were waiting for the next dance to begin when all of a sudden a small yapancha (tiny powerful whirlwind) developed in the dance area and swished rapidly in our direction. There was no way we could run fast enough to avoid it, so we and those near us were peppered with fine grains of sand in our hair, our eyes, mouth and nose. It saturated our fresh white clothes.

When we left the dance, dark-skinned and disheveled, our own mothers would not have recognized us.

Usually held during the winter months, the Matachines dance, as performed by New Mexico's Pueblos, is somewhat akin to the old English Morris dance and similar dances found in Spain, Italy and France.

Brought to New Mexico by the Spanish conquistadores, the new world version is based loosely on the Mexican tale of the conqueror Cortes and his love of the Princess Marina who was said to have been the Aztec Emperor Montezuma's daughter.

After it was introduced to the Pueblo Indians, they, being charmed by the sweet story and colorful costumes, copied it from the Spaniards and added it to their own repertoire.

La Malinche takes the part of the Princess, while Mananca portrays Montezuma. The line dancers are the Matachines and the abuelos and abuelas (grandfathers and grandmothers) are the clowns. Indian dances, no matter how solemn, always have clowns.

At Santa Ana Pueblo, where I saw the dance for the first time, the costumes were the Indians' conception of the original Spanish version.

On their heads, the Matachines wore tall mitres. The mitres were embellished with Christian symbols, beads and spangles, with two tall eagle feathers protruding from each. Colorful ribbons streamed down the back to the shoulders, and a black cloth mask covered the face to just below the nose. The chin and neck were concealed behind a bandana tied behind the head. A belt of jingling sleigh bells was fastened at the waist overlaying an embroidered cotton apron. Beaded buckskin trousers, moccasins, a long-sleeved white shirt and vest completed the costume. The dancers each carried a wooden sword-like piece in one hand and a gourd rattle in the other.

The clowns wore rags and, covering their faces, were horrible looking masks having huge ears, big noses and gaping mouths with big ugly fangs protruding. Their wigs were made from once-white rag floor mops.

Little *El Torro*, the bull, portrayed by a young boy, wore a buckskin with horns attached covering his body and sprouting from his head. He carried two sticks in front to support his crouching position.

La Malinche was dressed all in white with a veil and wreath of white flowers on her head.

The music began and the Matachines formed in two lines and danced in tricky, syncopated kick steps, first facing then crossing over to dance back again. Mananca danced back and forth, up and down the line, with La Malinche solemnly following. At the end of each set the shotgun was fired. The clowns yelled jokes and sometimes obscenities at the dancers and onlookers, and the bull butted them and attempted to butt the dancers. The dancers remained stoic, unmoved by the antics going on around them.

At the end, while the Matachines knelt, the little bull was roped and killed, the gun was fired, and the meat of the bull was symbolically distributed to the dancers, after which the bull revived and ran away to play another day.

After the dance, Marian and I were invited by Porfirio, the Governor, and his wife, Dora, to eat at their house. Dora was a pretty, older, little, round Indian woman and Porfirio was a garrulous old rogue. He loved to tell the story about the time he shot himself in his foot. He had started to clean his gun and, thinking he had removed all the bullets, had the gun pointed downward correctly to begin his cleaning operation when he pulled the trigger! Bang, it went off to his amazement. The single bullet which was still in the chamber went right through his boot and into his foot. "Now," he said, "I look in each chamber three times, and then I make sure the barrel is aimed at the floor and not at my foot before I pull the trigger!"

Dora was a great cook. She served the usual beans, chile and tortillas, but she had also made her sensational *chiles rellanos*. I had never eaten better. Hers were made with rice, cheese and piñon nuts formed in a tight ball, then coated with a green chile, lightly battered and deep-fried. Delicious!

Among winter festivities at the Pueblos is the Kings Day dance and give-away ritual held on January 6, 12th night or Epiphany. The dance is incidental to the hilarious events taking place from the rooftops surrounding the dance plaza.

All male inhabitants named Rey or Reyes (king or kings) mount the roof tops with bushels of produce and gifts which they exuberantly hurl to the crowd waiting below with arms outstretched. Loaves of bread, giant zucchini squash, boxes of Kleenex, oranges and lemons are tossed to the laughing crowd. Then rolls of toilet paper, unfurling in the breeze, fly through the air, wrapping around the branches of trees and the heads and bodies of onlookers, much to the giggling delight of all.

Suddenly we saw a live, squirming, protesting, crowing rooster flung to a happy bystander. Next came a clawing, yowling, wriggling, very incensed cat which landed unceremoniously on the head of a stunned, unsuspecting Navajo guest. That really brought forth shouts of approval and great guffaws from the Puebloans for the Navajo are noted spongers and are just tolerated at these affairs.

The give-away ritual can go on for hours depending upon the number of Rey and Reyes living in the Pueblo. Once the grabbing is over, there is a brief dance. Then all go home satisfied with the day and their loot.

The first animal dance I saw was at Tesuque Pueblo just a few miles north from the city. We had risen in the wee hours on a frigid morning in early February because we had to be at the Pueblo before sunrise. Marian, who had spent years in anthropology and knew all about Indian lore and customs, was shepherding a group of us which included her daughter-in-law and one-year-old granddaughter to the event. I drove into the dark pueblo and Marian directed me to a spot just off the road which she said would be a perfect place for us to watch. I parked the car and Marian got out to reconnoiter. Suddenly she rushed back to the car, got in and, appalled, said, "We've got to get out of here. The dancers are coming over the hill and the car is directly in their path. There'll be hell to pay if they catch us here!" Needless to say, we all got a good laugh at our great expert's expense, and she was teased unmercifully for the rest of the day—"Yeah, Marian, just the perfect spot!"

The animal dancers burst over the hill just as the sun crept into view over the Sangres. There were a couple of buffalos, clad in shaggy buffalo skins with horned head attached. Their bodies were painted black above and below their buckskin kilts. They carried gourd rattles and bows and arrows. The deer wore antlers on their heads with a fan-like arrangement of painted reeds in front. They wore the traditional

Hopi Kilts, white shirts with sashes and sleigh bells around their waists. Covering their legs were white lacey pantaloons tied under the knee with colorful yarn sashes. A pine bough framed each side of their blackened faces. They danced in a bent position, using two decorated sticks to signify their forelegs.

The hunter, wearing a buckskin suit with fringed trousers and a buckskin cape over his shoulders, carried a bow and arrows and joined the others.

The deer circled and danced to the rhythm of the drums and the chorus. Then they would stop and lean forward on their sticks, gazing first one way and then the other, looking for the hunter. The rhythm would change and the deer would dance toward the buffalo, back in a circle and then stop, bend forward on the sticks and again look this way and that for the hunter.

The Koshares came out, teased the dancers and poked fun at the onlookers. Then one of them spied a young woman with a camera. In unison, they jumped the poor girl and ripped the camera from her hands. Her eyes grew huge. I think she was afraid for her life. The Koshares removed the film from her camera and gave the camera back, but all of them made shame-on-you gestures, rubbing one index finger along the other, while making clacking noises with their tongues against their teeth. Mortified, the girl turned and fled the dance plaza.

We had had enough of the cold and were hungry and tired so we, too, went home.

19

Santa Feans generously open their homes and gardens for charitable events. This works best when you, the owner, have some control over who the guests are to be. We did not have the guest list the one time we offered our garden for a cocktail party benefit for one of the musical theatre organizations. We provided the bartender, drinks and canapes with the condition that it was to be an outdoor party and that guests would be guided from the front door to the patio door coming and going, with no lingering inside the house.

So much for conditions. We had even taken the precaution of closing off the bedroom wing and the master suite, or so we thought. The party started sedately enough with guests dutifully staying outside on the patio. Where this hoard of people came from, I do not know. We knew so many people in Santa Fe that it seemed impossible that there would not be one familiar face in the group, but such was the case. As the party progressed, I slipped inside the house to make sure all was in order. With so many strangers about, that seemed prudent. To my dismay and great annoyance, not only did I discover the bedroom wing open, but I further found people prowling in the rooms, opening drawers, looking in closets, touching, picking up and putting down our possessions. I finally said as calmly and politely as I could, "What are you people doing inside? The party, drinks, food are all outside."

Nobody paid the slightest heed. They all just continued with what they were doing. Distraught and mad, I stomped back outside, went directly to the bartender and told him to close the bar in five minutes. I then found the organizer of the event and told him he had fifteen minutes to round up his guests and get them out of there—and nastily, "Don't forget those goons in the house that are busily exploring our bedrooms, closets and dressers that you vowed not to let happen."

We certainly picked the wrong charity to befriend because most of our friends who have opened their houses have had much more pleasant experiences.

Our good friend, Wally Sargent, and his wife, Leese, loved to give big parties whether or not it was to support a charity. They had a great house for parties—very large, built in a U shape, the right side of which was shorter than the other. It was situated way up the canyon off the back road that led to Tesuque. Snuggly settled amid a forest of pine and aspen, the house had on its inside walls a treasure trove of fine paintings by early Taos and Santa Fe artists. The large living room was backed by an almost equally large music room with a grand piano which Wally played. There was a lavish master suite and an entire wing for the children off and away from the living area. Outside in the center of the U was a large kidney shaped swimming pool surrounded on two sides by flagstone walks and a sitting area and, in the summer, with lush green grass on the other two sides. At big summertime parties, there was a bar at the foot of the left or long side of the U and another at the right or shorter side of the U, thus making the two bars diagonally across the pool from each other.

We were there for a charitable function given to benefit the Film Festival, I believe. Anyway, there were a number of Hollywood types there, so that's what it must have been. I remember talking to Lillian Gish at length. She was a delightful, wispy, elderly lady who exuded a sort of old-world charm. She spoke of her experiences on stage and in the movies with fondness and gentle humor. Katy Jarrado, who had been a slim, fiery, attractive character actress in the 1930s and 40s, had ballooned into a big, bawdy broad; and Ginger Rogers, trying to cling to her youthful good looks only made herself look coarse and rather pathetic. The latter two stars were quite a contrast to the sedate Lillian Gish.

After my conversation with Miss Gish, I wandered over to the bar at the short end of the pool and, after a good wait, finally got a drink. I turned from the bar and started back to where Marian, still talking to Lillian Gish, was sitting on the patio in the center of the U, when I almost ran into a big, rugged-looking man who only could be Charlton Heston. I stopped to chat and he said to me, "This bar is too busy; how do I get to that bar over there!" I've never been given to quick quips, so I don't know how it happened that, unbidden, the answer rolled out of my mouth, "Why, you just part the waters and walk right over there?" The old, humorless stiff-neck didn't even smile—just turned on his heel and walked to the near bar. Well, I scampered over and told the story to Marian and Miss Gish, and the three of us had a good laugh.

20

In the late 1970s, Santa Fe's Chamber of Commerce began to be very actively involved in pursuing events that would publicize the city. In 1979, it succeeded in luring the Perry Como Christmas Show to Santa Fe for the show's production that year. I think Perry Como was beloved throughout the world, but I discovered he certainly was in Santa Fe.

Blasé elderly ladies, who normally would not have walked across the street to see a celebrity, clamored for a chance to participate or even to watch a scene being filmed. Marian and I were active in the Chamber of Commerce at the time and were able to get the Jones sisters, Hester and Ellen, and my mother choice seats in Cristo Rey Church for the scene that took place there.

The three ole gals were having the time of their lives enthusiastically singing Christmas carols, unaware that the camera had panned in their direction until the program was aired on TV. They called after the show, ecstatic, "Did you see us? We were in the show!" Worldly-wise elderly dames were not as apathetic as they thought they were.

The past-president of the Chamber, Walt Chapman, and his wife, Joan, hosted a party in their home for the cast when the production was finished. Their house was so jammed with invitees and gate-crashers (acceptable in Santa Fe) that a person was lucky to find a square foot of space in which to stand—movement was limited. Perry Como was a shy man, and he seemed to be completely overwhelmed. He disappeared the second he discovered a get-away path. We happened to have found our niche in the only room in which he appeared. Others didn't get a glimpse of him.

Another promotional event in which the Chamber of Commerce was substantially involved was New York's Lord & Taylor's *Focus America*. We wined and dined the group sent out by the store to make the final choice of the three cities still in the running to be featured in their big affair.

Marian and I gave a catered party for them in our business studio which totally bombed. We had a handsome bartender who offered drinks before dinner. Each of the guests ordered Perrier water; one was so bold as to order his with lime. We sat down to a beautiful dinner—filet mignon with fresh mushrooms, asparagus with hollandaise, and tiny new potatoes in butter and parsley, preceded by a small Caesar salad and followed with vanilla ice cream topped with fresh strawberries. I guess they were all on diets. Not one of them ate more than three bites of the entree, nor more than a couple bites of the salad and dessert. What a waste! Their lack of enthusiasm for our dinner party made us uneasy about Santa Fe's chances of being chosen.

Our worries proved to be baseless, and Santa Fe was chosen. What a boon to the city's economy and for the artisans whose work would be displayed and sold in Lord & Taylor's New York store—dress designers, potters, wood-carvers, weavers, jewelers, doll-makers and even chile-jelly producers would benefit.

The town was alive with activity, preparing for the big event. The grand opening was to take place in New York in April, 1982, and hundreds of Santa Feans were zealously planning to attend.

The big day arrived, and three hundred eager patriots flew to New York the day before. We awoke the next morning to a white world—the city had been blanketed with ten inches of snow during the night! That didn't dampen the spirits of hardy Santa Feans, but it did discourage New Yorkers, which severely limited attendance. One Lord & Taylor employee was heard to comment, "Thank goodness for all these crazy Santa Feans. Without them, this place would have been a morgue tonight!"

The Santa Fe Festival of the Arts was conceived by the Santa Fe Chamber of Commerce to celebrate ALL of the arts in Santa Fe; however, it became obvious almost immediately that that was a too far-reaching project, and so it was limited to the visual arts. Even limited, it became a daunting undertaking. There were to be art shows in almost every major hotel in town; the museum would have a show, and the grandest of them all would be a gigantic invitational at the Convention Center.

The planning, organization, committees and numbers of people needed to pull it off was mind-boggling. The biggest task of all was the funding. An enormous amount of money would be needed and, faced with the dilemma of how to get it, the Chamber decided it would have to set up a separate entity that could qualify for non-profit status so that donations could be solicited, grants could be sought, and benefit schemes could be pursued.

The most successful benefit concocted was the Non-Artist Art Show and Auction. This turned out to be a measure of "robbing Peter to pay Paul" in that most of the non-artists entering the show were committee members, and most of the bidding participants were those same committee members. Drinks flowed freely at these affairs to loosen inhibitions and pocketbooks—which they did. It was a hilarious, hysterical evening with everyone bidding fantastic amounts for bizarre objets d'art. To put this in perspective, it is necessary to remember that this was in the high-living, loose-spending, devil-may-care 80s.

One year, just a few days before the auction was to be held, a bunch of us were having drinks in Wally Sargent's hotel room where we were winding up a Chamber of Commerce retreat. Wally, who was that year's President of the Festival of the Arts, complained that he hadn't done his painting for the auction and he didn't have any ideas on what to do and no time to do it. Somebody grabbed one of those modern, artsy-type, make-a-statement magazines that usually enjoyed a brief honeymoon of popularity from the coffee table. Thumbing through it, he found a page printed in bright red devoid of printing—just a bright red, otherwise blank page. He very carefully tore it out of the magazine and handed it to Wally. "Just run your signature across the center of this page, have it framed and your art entry is ready for the auction." Wally's signature was undecipherable. It looked a bit like a scrawled peacock with head down and tail feather angled upward. He did as he was told and had the result framed and hung at the auction. Several inebriated, happy-go-lucky, big spenders bid that framed magazine page with a scribble on it up to $450! The Non-Artist Art Auction was the best fund-raiser of the Festival.

The Santa Fe Festival of the Arts was a grand ballyhoo and, in many ways, successful. But it required titanic effort and devotion that, after four years—when the original organizers were no longer on the board of the Chamber and the younger blood didn't have the heart for it—the Festival passed into oblivion.

21

I think Santa Feans always have had a love affair with adobe and an obsession with building, remodeling, restoring, taking out and adding on. We all have tried our hand at it at least once.

In the late 1970s, Marian and I bought a small native-built adobe on the west side because we had a little money ahead and it seemed like a good investment. We had searched the classifieds until we came upon one that seemed a likely candidate. We wanted cheap—and it was. We wanted adobe—and it said it was. It also said it was three bedrooms, kitchen, dining room, living room, bath and even a small cellar.

We called the realtor and went looking. The rooms were tiny and, when I knocked on one of the walls, there was a hollow sound, not like adobe at all. I asked the realtor, "Are you sure this is adobe?" Of course," he replied, "the man's wife wanted squared corners so he covered the adobe with stud walls." "And the ceilings," Marian queried, "Are there vigas under the wallboard?" He assured us there were, so we bought it.

The interior was a mess, and the exterior plaster was so bad and had been repaired so many times it looked like a patchwork quilt.

And the yard was god-awful, but it was a nice, big corner lot and as I said—it was cheap!

A friend of ours, who had had a lot of experience building, came over for a look shortly after we had bought our prize. He commented, "Bulldoze it!"

Undaunted by that caustic remark, we started tearing out with help from a group of nice young men we had sort of picked up off the street. First, the adobe wall between two of the bedrooms came down; then wallboard flew off and studs were pried out; then the ceiling board came down. There were vigas but, to our amazement, they didn't support the roof. The vigas were parallel to the floor, but the roof wasn't! It rose from a line even with the vigas at the outside edge to a peak ten inches above at the other end, with nothing but empty space between. So why were the vigas there at all? Of course, the old man had used them to support the fake ceiling. Much to our regret, there was no alternative but to take a skill saw and cut them down.

In the now big room that had been two of the bedrooms, we decided to build a corner fireplace. The floors were wood and even I knew they wouldn't support an adobe fireplace, so I told one of the workmen to cut a hole in the floor and build a solid support, using pumice blocks and poured cement. The next day when I went by, I discovered him busily arranging pumice blocks with wet cement on TOP of the floor. I yelled at him to get that mess off the floor pronto and, as soon as he finished, I told him to get out and not to come back. After that we hired a pair of known fireplace builders to do the job.

Before the ceiling board was pulled down in the front rooms, we hired an electrician to come in and throw new lines into that part of the house. There was a horrid chandelier in the dining room which the electrician decided to use to pull one of his lines through. He got on his ladder and began to take the fixture down. As he pulled it away, a very dead mouse fell in the startled man's face.

After the stud walls were removed, the old plaster covering the adobe bricks had to be pulled off to enable us to rewire. What an incredible amount of rubble we accumulated. In some places in the front part of the house, we found patches of plaster six inches thick.

We decided to put another fireplace in the corner of what was now the long front room. We wanted a stepped raised hearth of flagstone, with bancos built in on each side, and the stepped area was to be kidney-shaped at the base. To prepare the area for our fireplace builders, we needed to tear out some of the floor and build a base to the ground below. I drew a line on the floor in the kidney shape which the workmen were to follow when removing the floor boards. Later that day, I returned to find two workmen on their hands and knees gleefully pulling out the floor without any regard to the line I had drawn—in fact, they had already ripped out beyond where the line had been. Alas, we lost the kidney shape, but at least I caught them before they'd torn out the entire floor.

Plastering adobe is a complicated and tedious process. First, all of the adobe bricks must be firmly wired with chicken wire. Next, the first coat, this one of cement, is applied. After it is set, another coat is put on and then, finally, the coat of smooth plaster finishes the job. After the last coat has dried and all is completely cured, painting begins.

Marian and I put two coats of white paint throughout. And we spent hours polishing the flagstone steps to the fireplace—first with a coat of red shoe polish, then a coat of black, then another coat of red and black until we had rubbed and polished four coats—but it was handsome. In fact, as much to our surprise as to the friend who had made the nasty comment about bulldozing, the house within a year was truly a charmer and totally unrecognizable from its previous form.

Mike Fischer was captivated with adobe and the remarkable design elements that could be achieved through its use. I don't know whatever became of Mike but, while he was designing and building adobe homes, he created magical castles for ordinary people.

Mike grew up on Mercer Island in Washington State and was introduced to Santa Fe when he was a teenage Eagle Scout on his way to Philmont Boy Scout Ranch in Cimarron, New Mexico. He was dazzled by Santa Fe's soft-lined, free-flowing adobe buildings and imagined himself as a designer and builder of adobe homes. He knew then what his life's ambition was to be.

After he got his architectural degree from Washington University, Mike married. He and his wife bolted from the dreary, cloudy skies of Washington to the sunny and vivid blue skies of Santa Fe where he intended to seek fulfillment of his dream to design and build adobe homes.

He succeeded. At the last count I knew, Mike had built more than twenty Santa Fe style houses and condominiums, and remodeled dozens more. A great believer, supporter and follower of Santa Fe's Historic Styles Ordinance, Mike considered that architecture was the most important visual element in Santa Fe's culture and stoutly defended his opinion.

Mike used the traditional features of Santa Fe style which, architecturally, is a conglomerate of Pueblo-Indian, Spanish custom and individual innovation, and incorporated his own twists into the final product.

Traditional features include vigas, latillas, exposed lintels above doors and windows, beehive fireplaces, tile embellishments, and floors of flagstone, brick, slate or poured adobe. To Mike, it was essential that there be no sraight lines. Hand-plastered walls, which included a lot of curves, were vital. He would fashion semi-enclosed spaces by erecting curved, stepped walls around an entryway or to define a kitchen. He would merge rooms with a hint of separation created through an architectural device such as using a two-faced, raised-hearth fireplace in double beehive shape to divide a living room from a dining room. He made liberal use of wood throughout his houses, with accents of massive carved wood supports strategically placed for both sturdiness and eye appeal.

Wherever Mike went and whatever he may be doing, he left a legacy of lovingly-sculpted Santa Fe style homes behind.

Zig and Stephanie Kosicki bought a small adobe house—one bedroom, bath, living room and kitchen—on upper Garcia Street and began adding. First they converted the existing portal into a bedroom and a small hot house; then they added a spacious entryway and, off it and up a short flight of steps, a master bedroom, bath and dressing room. Their property was hilly, sloping this way and that; and, as was customary in Santa Fe, homes were built with the lay of the land instead of excavating to make everything on one level.

Off the entryway in the opposite direction from the bedroom, they added an enormous high-ceilinged living room which ran perpendicularly to the entry and the added master suite. The living room was more than 40 feet long and perfectly proportioned at a little more than 20 feet wide.

At the far end of the living room, a flight of steps, parallel to the entry, descended to the dining room off of which was the kitchen.

The Kosickis were avid collectors, and the house was stuffed with Indian artifacts, Spanish Colonial religious icons, modern paintings and sculpture.

The house, near the top of Garcia Street hill, lay in the path of the Museum of New Mexico's walking tour route. The Kosickis had a tall flag pole at the front of their property from which a regulation size flag always flew. One day Stephanie was startled by a group of about twenty German nuns who surged through her front door and, without as much as a greeting to her, roamed about her house, fingering her treasures and commenting to one another in German. When they finished their thorough inspection of her house and belongings, they waltzed out the front door without a word. Stephanie. bemused by the peculiar happening, locked the front door after them and vowed to herself to keep it locked. She noticed in the old holy water font kept by the window a sprinkling of dimes and nickles—largess from the sisters!

Douglas Johnson, self-pronounced 13th Century man, artist of meticulously-rendered, Indian-influenced illusionary paintings, was a builder of cliff dwellings which he did in classic pueblo style. Marian and I visited him in his first home in the cliffs. Neither of us was very young—certainly not as young as Douglas, nor as small nor as agile. It took all our nerve to climb his ladder up that treacherous cliff face to reach his wee home. The front entrance suddenly loomed in front of Marian when she reached the top of the ladder. The entrance was small, more the size of a window than a door, and one had to traverse a high lip over which inside there were steps below. Marian tried to maneuver herself inside, swore a little and tried again. She swore a little more and squawked at me that she couldn't do it. I was right behind her on the ladder, none too happy with my position or with the cold wind blowing, so I gave her a nice, firm push. She plopped inside like a cork out of a champagne bottle and sprawled unceremoniously upside down on her behind at Douglas' feet. He, of course, was laughing uproariously. Next, I tried to get in. I got as far as to have one leg over the lip, dangling inside and puzzling over what would be my next move when Marian, who had righted herself, grabbed my leg with one hand and my hand that was tentatively clinging to the smooth side of the entrance hole with her other hand. With a strong jerk from her, I tumbled in to land undignifiedly in as awkward a position as she had. And all the time, that scamp Douglas was laughing his head off.

I had thought of being able to stand up once inside. Wrong! Even Douglas, who was small and Marian, who was about the same height, could only stand upright in the back of the room because the roof sloped downward from back to front to allow melting snow and rain to run off.

It was a midget-sized, sweet, cozy place with a corner beehive fireplace, built-in shelves for his books, and Navajo rugs on the floor. The other room was his bedroom and it had been made from an existing recess in the face of the rock wall.

The little cliff house was beautifully built, with carefully-laid native stone mortared with adobe plaster. The ceiling was made of latillas (peeled slender aspen branches) laid side-by-side supported by vigas (large peeled pine trees) and overlaid with bushels of dirt from which a few cacti had emerged.

Douglas had lived among the Navajo in Canyon de Chelly for a number of years and became immersed in Indian ways. He later visited the Indian ruins in Chaco Canyon and at Mese Verde, and was fascinated by intricate stone work at Chaco and the cliff dwellings at Mesa Verde. His paintings and his way of life are the result of these influences.

Douglas, who owns fifteen acres in a remote corner of Northern New Mexico, later built another, more elaborate dwelling on a south-facing cliff to take advantage of the solar possibilities. This one has larger rooms, slightly higher ceilings, and two stories, but is constructed with banded stonework in classic Chaco Canyon style. Douglas' way of life is not for everyone and, as he said to us when he finally quit laughing, "It's a good thing I'm young!" "You bet it is !"

22

You can know things intellectually without processing them internally, and so it was hard for me to believe that Santa Fe and its environs really had been under water—part of an inland sea. I could not accept that notion until Marian took me fossil hunting up on Cerro Gordo Road where the road swoops north from Canyon Road to meet Cerro Gordo—a place I had been many times without realizing its significance in the earth's development.

What treasures we found embedded in chunks of rock, flat scraps of sandstone and even lying loose on the ground. Fossilized sea worms and seashells of all sizes and description came into focus on careful scrutiny. The findings were almost beyond comprehension. Here we stood at what today is some 7500 feet above sea level in the midst of what many millennia before had been a vast ocean.

When the seas receded, dinosaurs roamed what was to become Santa Fe. Parts of the remains of Stegosaurus and bones of Diplodocus, a gigantic beast some 90 feet long, standing 15 feet tall and weighing in at 20 tons, were found just off Palace Avenue and north of Cerro Gordo Road.

We didn't find anything that exotic, but we did find a fossilized mollusk about the size of a dinner plate in circumference on one of our forays and, on another, the remnants of the leg bone of an ancestor of today's rhinoceros.

I discovered that camels once had been indigenous to New Mexico when we went to see the Camel Tracks, a marked area set aside as a sort of minor monument a little drive southwest of the city limits. Escaping from an erupting volcano, camels had left imprints of their hooves in soft, cooling lava which had hardened and preserved their escape route for all time.

Further evidence left by the dromedaries has been found just off the highway at a roadside curiosity stop a few miles north of the city. A bulging sandstone ridge called Camel Rock has eroded through time into a shape that is remarkably like that of a kneeling camel and, equally remarkable, fossilized bone fragments and teeth of prehistoric camels have been found at that site.

A man I knew, Larry Wilson, had a granddaughter who was so enamored of dinosaurs during the recently past dinosaur craze, that he made his yard into a dinosaur zoo for her.

Larry, a roofer by trade, did marvelous things for Santa Fe's roofs with polyurethane foam. Then, urged by his granddaughter, his vocation melded into an avocation when he began sculpting life-size dinosaurs. He made the armatures of rebar and screen which he sprayed generously with polyurethane foam. He carved the foam to shape details and produced Tyrannosaurus Rex, a Triceratops—the fellow that caused such havoc in *Jurassic Park*—Pterodactyl and Stegosaurus, all of which he had placed in his front yard. Naturally, his unique menagerie became a tourist attraction and every kid for miles around wanted to see and play on his dinosaurs.

On another outing, Marian was driving her VW and we were approaching the Cerrillos Hills, about 20 miles south of Santa Fe, trying to locate an old abandoned turquoise mine. Suddenly, Marian swerved off the road into an arroyo (a dry river bed) which sloped lazily upward. The little car bounced over rocks, shimmied through patches of sand and, as the going got steeper, gasped a bit as it slogged steadily upward. By the side of the arroyo, a crudely printed sign read Meadows Gold. "Humph," I commented to Marian, "what's a dairy doing out here, way off in the boonies?" Marian simply replied, "It doesn't seem likely." And we continued surging upward. I belatedly realized that the midwestern dairy, Meadow Gold, didn't have an "S." All at once the car burst over the edge and on top of level ground, and we sat facing two buildings—one long, low building in front of us and the other adjacent to the first, but built up from a gully in two stories—with another "Meadows Gold" sign over both. In the somewhat eerie silence, we sat pondering what this might be. Marian, not one to ponder long, jumped out of the car and shouted, "Come on, let's see what we've found." I, being of a more cautious bent, said "Maybe we'd better hightail it out of here!" "Ah, come on, where's your spirit of adventure?" she taunted. So we approached the door of the nearest building when, abruptly, it popped open and there stood an elderly, distinguished-looking man, pipe in hand and wearing one of those black protective aprons. He eyed us fixedly, then shyly smiled and said softly, "What brings you here?" Marian, with her customary bravado, replied, "We came to find out what goes on here and what Meadows Gold might be."

His eyes twinkled, he held out his hand and asserted, "You've come to the right man. I'm Dr. Zausenhaus. Come, I'll show you around and explain what I'm doing here."

I was hesitant, but Marian boldly strode over, shook his hand and exclaimed, "We'd like that." So I shook his hand and followed, albeit not as eagerly.

He took us through his office and down a long ramp to the ground level of the other building which proved to be only one story with a very high ceiling and a mass of high, large windows all around the periphery so that the building was full of light. It was also full of huge vats and tumblers with a complicated arrangement of pipes snaking overhead and between the vats. The whole place looked like a page out of a science fiction novel. Dr. Zausenhaus began explaining the functions of each piece of equipment, but the gist of it was that the geologists with Meadows Gold, which was a metallic survey company, had discovered traces of precious metals such as iridium, lithium, palladium and plutonium—all iums in the Cerrillos rocks. The Doctor was attempting to create an efficient way of extracting those that would be viable commercially.

After listening to his spiel for a polite period and when he seemed to be winding down, we took our leave. Poor man—I think he was very lonely working there all alone day after day.

We got back in the car, headed north along the ridge, and came at last to an old turquoise mine. It was a great hole in the earth exposed to the daylight so we could look down and see the leavings of what had once been a vein of turquoise. We found a few scraps lying half-hidden in the grasses and weeds, as well as a couple of pretty nice pieces. Cerrillos turquoise is characterized by its distinctive green color and, because all of the Cerrillos mines have been played out, it is a rare find.

While there, we noticed off in the distance a two-story, Victorian-style brick house sitting isolated on a slight rise. How strange, I thought, to see a brick house or any house out here. "Marian, let's drive over there and take a closer look at that house." Marian thought a moment and remarked, "I seem to remember hearing something about that house. Umm, yes—an Englishman came over from London, became smitten with this country and, thinking there was surely gold in them thar hills, bought some land, built the house, sent for his family, and began his search for riches. As the story goes, his wife arrived, found the area quite desolate, disliked the house and thought her husband mad. She took the children and fled back to merry old England. Her husband hung on for a while, seeking a strike. Finally, disenchanted and despondent, he gave up and returned to England."

When we got a closer look at the house, it was a forlorn image of its former grace. Window glass was broken or gone with only a few jagged pieces here and there. The door hung loosely from its mooring, and the wood was pockmarked from the repeated clashes of sand and rain. Even the bricks were marred and bitten by sand. The interior was a shambles of dust, debris and shattered furniture. It was a demoralizing testimony to a man's broken dream. "Let's get out of here!" we cried to each other in unison, and so we did.

Thanksgiving was the occasion for our excursion to Truchas, a village high in the mountains about 25 miles northeast of Santa Fe. Marian's oldest son, John, and his wife, Caroline, were living in a rustic cabin a couple of miles beyond the village limit and were preparing a feast for us.

It was a cold, blustery day with the feel of snow in the air as we wound our way up the steep mountain road which veers off to the east from the main Taos Highway. As we approached the village, the first tentative flakes of snow greeted us. On we went, watching the frolicking waters dancing through the acequia (irrigation ditch) alongside the road. We got to the entrance to their place and crossed the little bridge over the acequia. The water looked so pure and clean and cold.

The cabin was constructed of logs chinked with adobe mortar and with the interior walls plastered and painted white. Escaping smoke from the fireplace and wood stove had tinted the walls more gray than white in the long room which served as living, dining and kitchen. At one end was the fireplace and, at the other the wood stove and sink with a cold water pump arrangement.

There were other guests, a doctor and his wife whom we knew and another couple. I couldn't imagine cooking Thanksgiving dinner for two, let alone for eight, in those primitive conditions, but John and Caroline did.

On a wood stove, she had baked a huge, beautifully browned turkey, cooked creamed onions from their garden, made dressing, candied yams, mashed potatoes, gravy, hot biscuits and two kinds of pie—minced meat and pumpkin. That took fortitude and talent. With a roaring fire in the fireplace crackling merrily and snow falling gently outside, we sat down to a fabulous dinner. I felt like a pilgrim—and later a very stuffed pilgrim.

After dinner, we sang songs and told stories. It was a time of true togetherness without interruption from television, telephone or even radio. Fulfilled from a Thanksgiving like no other we had ever experienced, we inched down the mountain and home.

23

Christmas in Santa Fe is old-fashioned, home-spun and communal. Multicolored, tiny electric lights sparkle among the branches of the trees in the central plaza. Fresh, live pine boughs with jumbo red velvet bows wrap the round vigas supporting the portales on the four streets surrounding the plaza, as well as those up Palace Avenue fronting Prince Patio and Sena Plaza. Outlining the parapets of all the major downtown buildings are *farolitos*.

Luminarias are a more recognizable word for most of the general public, because misguided Albuquerqueans incorrectly tagged *farolitos*—which are the small sand-seated, candle-nested brown bags—as *luminarias;* whereas *luminarias* are actually small bonfires made by cross-hatching short splits of pitch-filled, fast-burning piñon logs in a square shape with an empty center. The little bonfires were introduced to the Pueblo Indians by the Spanish Franciscans in the mid-16th Century to enhance their Christmas celebratory dances, but farolitos came into vogue much later.

Delicate paper lanterns imported from the Far East were in use in Mexico but not available in the remote land-locked inhabited regions of New Mexico. It wasn't until the invention of the square-bottomed, brown paper sack in Boston in the late 19th Century that the wherewithal to create farolitos became available to New Mexicans.

Since that time, the little brown, amber-glowing lights have been used by Santa Feans to mark special occasions and, most particularly, Christmas Eve. The tradition began to falter toward the middle of the 20th Century because it became increasingly difficult for the owners of large several-storied buildings—with numerous setbacks, balconies and cupolas—to find cheap labor to prepare, place and light the little lanterns. That, combined with anxious insurance companies' concerns regarding potential fire hazards, almost surely would have portended the death knell to *farolitos* on commercial buildings had it not been for the fortuitous invention in the 1970s of electrified *farolitos*.

Although purists scorned the use of electrified *farolitos*, a tradition was saved. Today, during the Christmas season, the entire downtown glows with the amber lanterns radiating from every parapet, balcony and cupola.

On Christmas Eve, traditional farolitos are placed along the walkways in the Plaza and lighted by the Boy Scouts. Private homes throughout the city are aglow with flickering candle-sacks as they compete in the Old Santa Fe Association's traditional lighting contest.

According to the Association's rules, no electric lights can be visible outside or inside the houses, so there is a silent darkness broken only by the illumination from the farolitos and the *luminarias*. The little bonfires have been placed at frequent intervals by considerate homeowners to provide warmth and cheer to the foot travelers. At many of the fires, tables have been set with trays of *biscochitos* (anise-flavored sugar cookies) and cauldrons of hot spiced wine or Mexican hot chocolate. Often groups will gather for warmth and sustenance and will favor the neighborhood with Christmas carols.

Marian and I were selected by the Old Santa Fe Association to judge the contest two years in a row. The first year, it was a bitter cold night, and we drove from one end of town to the other, viewing the entries. There was a three-story Victorian house that sat high on a hill above downtown Santa Fe which was adorned with gingerbread and bric-a-brac of the era and had been painstakingly outlined with *farolitos*. The display was thrilling, and we thought our quest for the first place award had ended. When I pulled the car around a curve in the road to get a better look at the front of the house—Ouch!—the large front window on the first floor was ablaze with multi-colored twinkling electric lights wrapped around a giant Christmas tree. The rest of the house was dark, but someone had forgotten the Christmas tree; and this magnificent spectacle was instantly disqualified. We found another almost-equally spectacular show way up Canyon Road to award first prize.

The following year was easy. The people in the Victorian house remembered to turn off all of their electric lights, and they won first place hands down.

Then it was home to a big pot of posole simmering on the back of the stove. Posole, hominy cooked in chicken broth with pork, and spiced with red chile, oregano, onion and garlic, is to Christmas Eve in Santa Fe what black-eyed peas are to New Years in other parts of the country.

The last time we made the pilgrimage to the Canyon Road Christmas Eve Farolito extravaganza, cars were allowed to make the trip up the road. Everyone on the road, residences and businesses alike, goes all-out with *farolitos* lining the parapets, the gables, cupolas, window ledges, outlining doorways and walkways along the curbs; and some of the more enterprising even lined large tree limbs. Early in the evening, there were no electric lights to be seen, and the street was a wondrous pageant to look upon. Later, gallery owners, other businesses and many residences turned on their lights and opened their doors to party time for everyone—mixed drinks, mulled wine, eggnog, hot chocolate, canapes, biscochitos and *empaniditas* (little half-moon-shaped minced meat pies) all were given freely to the revelers.

Christmas trees came in two varieties—those you bought and those you borrowed. This year we were looking for one to borrow.

We drove to a deserted, unfenced area not far from downtown to look for a large, shapely piñon tree to take home. It was a snowy day in mid-December with an accumulation of about six inches of snow on the ground, but we were not to be deterred. I was driving and looking, but Marian had the advantage of looking while not driving. Suddenly she whooped delightedly, "Stop the car. There's our tree just over there," pointing at a good-sized specimen only about 20 feet off the road.

It looked about right from where we stood by the car, so we got our axes out of the trunk and stalked over to where it stood. I was dubious when I realized it was considerably taller than I had thought, and it had a trunk that was at least five inches in diameter. "Do you think we can get this thing into the trunk?" I asked. "Of course." Marian was completely confident. "Gosh, it's awfully full," I sighed, troubled. "Yes, it's really a beauty," she sang happily. I whacked, she whacked; I chopped, she chopped—there's nothing easy about trying to cut down a sap-full, moisture-laden piñon tree. After what seemed hours, we had finally made inroads and, with a good push, it went down. We tugged and pulled, and finally got the brute to the car. Fortunately, the trunk of the car was big. We finally levered the cut trunk up on the bumper, then both with a mighty heave, pushed it up over the lip. We wiggled and shoved, and wobbled and shook, and heaved and wiggled it some more, and finally had the trunk end of the tree as far back in the trunk of the car as it could go—more than half of the upper branches stuck out over the lip of the trunk. No way were we going to get the lid closed. So in the car and away we drove, not fast and very careful of bumps and other obstacles in the dirt road because one good jolt and that monster would probably leap right out of the car.

Tree decorations in Santa Fe are more imaginative than in most other parts of the country. We had a fine mix of baubles from our respective youths—hand-carved wooden figurines by native Spanish craftsmen, wee Mexican dolls, Indian artifacts and elaborate hand-made ornaments. We used lots of multi-colored lights which are a pain to put on a big, full tree and the cause of many a household argument during the season. We hung our many baubles—a few fake red chiles, plenty of colorful dough-bread figures, a stuffed mouse with Santa hat lying atop a sled, a straw angel, a tiny stuffed burro, a kangaroo with Santa hat, old-fashioned brocaded St. Nicks, little soft Mexican dolls, wooden crosses and angels, a pressed tin owl and a cat, a number of White House annual commemorative decorations (which Marian's half-sister who lived in the Washington, D.C., area sent every year), miniature Indian sand paintings and head dresses, and a bunch of gaudy hand-made baubles created by our friend, Jean Hafemann, who snatched up costume jewelry as voraciously as a hungry locust in a cornfield, which she then assembled into flashy doodads for her friends.

The final effect was as multi-cultured as Santa Fe itself, and we gazed at it proudly and adoringly.

Marian and I sold *The Santa Fean* in 1994, retired and spent the next several years seeing the world. The millennium New Year arrived with Marian in the hospital fighting double pneumonia. She lost her battle and died January 5, 2000. With her death, I knew my sojourn in Santa Fe had come to an end. It was time for me to leave my beloved city, but I was confident that those who came after would find "my city different" just as captivating as I had found it half a century before.

www.ingramcontent.com/pod-product-compliance
Lightning Source LLC
Chambersburg PA
CBHW021015090426
42738CB00007B/795